The Sun Still Rises:

My Secrets for Survival

By Gail Gray Dove

Published by Richter Publishing LLC
www.richterpublishing.com

Book Cover Design: Tara Richter

Book Formatting & Photo Editing: Tara Richter & Sophia Gerneck

Editors: Abigail Bunner, Austin Hatch, Lux Figueroa, Sophia Gerneck, Adriana Hartman & Heather Pickert

Photos: by Gail Gray Dove

ISBN-13:978-1-954094-66-6

DISCLAIMER

DEDICATION

This book is dedicated to my daughters, my medical professionals, and those people who may feel they are experiencing significant obstacles in life and need renewed strength, resilience, and resourcefulness.

For my daughters, may you find the strength to persevere in times of difficulty. Always remember that you come from a family that did not have it easy, did not come from money, but were rich in strength and wisdom. They worked hard for what they accomplished and never gave up when things got tough. Their example should always be a beacon of light that draws you toward success in whatever you attempt to do. Just like your ancestors, you have the magic within you and the background of your faith to see you through anything that gets in the way of your happiness.

For my medical professionals, all I can say is "Thank You" for your knowledge, guidance, and dedication to your profession. Your hard work has been a direct benefit to my healing. I highly respect all of you. I am grateful to have had a team so supportive and technically gifted. I will never forget your compassion or the patience you have shown me.

For others who may be experiencing any obstacle in life where you are searching for hope or miracles, I encourage you to take the short journey through this story. This is my personal story of survival. I pray it helps you, even if only in the smallest way. This is my only reason for publishing it. For you, I wish you a renewed spirit that will carry you through your situation.

ACKNOWLEDGMENTS

I want to acknowledge God and my amazing family and friends.

To God, You guided me, listened to me when I didn't think I could go on, and performed miracles for me when I had little hope. You encouraged me through Your Word throughout my life and opened Your arms to me when I looked to You for strength and answers. You gifted me with two beautiful daughters who have enriched my life in ways I cannot describe. I am truly blessed.

To Mom and Dad, you demonstrated a work ethic that went above and beyond the norm; you taught me self-discipline, confidence, and endurance, always holding me accountable. These lessons have served me well in life so far. You supported me as I went through some of the most difficult stages in life. For these lessons, I could never repay you. I am forever grateful.

I hold abundant gratefulness for my daughter, Dianna. You generously and continually adjusted your schedule to take me to so many appointments, procedures, and surgeries that I lost count. You were my memory at each doctor's appointment and following each treatment and surgery that weakened my mind and body. You cleaned my home and grocery shopped because I couldn't, so that I had what I needed when I could not drive myself. I am also grateful to my daughter, Jennifer. You were always a phone call away, though you had a job and family and did not live locally. You listened to my progress reports and encouraged me when my spirits were low. I am so appreciative that you would sacrifice your vacation time to come and spend a week with me, although I could only sleep most of the time. I am genuinely thankful for you.

I love you both with all my heart.

To Uncle Wayne, though all of my uncles were treasures, you were a constant in my life during my most critical years. I looked up to you as an example of what I wanted to be. You were unbiased in my eyes, and I believe you may not have known how much of a difference that made. I love you for being there for me when I needed it most.

To my sister, Sue. You are a treasure to me. You are irreplaceable. This is not just because you have selflessly dropped whatever you were doing in more than one or two situations just to help me. It is also because I can't imagine not having *you* as my sister. The fun we had as kids, the banter and arguments, playing house with our dolls and digging tunnels in the snow, collecting treasures along the babbling brook, and, as adults, having a natural ability to support each other without hesitation, looking past our differences to honor each other for our uniqueness. As a child, I wanted to be just like you. Now I see the beauty of our differences. In our uniqueness, I see the beauty of Mom and Dad's attributes in both of us, and it makes me smile. I could not love you more.

To my brother, Glenn. You are also a treasure to me. I highly value that we have a love for God in common. You have a very soft heart like Mom, and you have the comedic nature of Dad. You make me laugh with no effort at all. You can light up the world with your sense of humor. So, keep sharing it with others. Laughing is healing. I love you with all my heart.

To my brother-in-law, Gordon (Dean), you may not be blood, but that really couldn't matter less to me. You have done so many things to help me, and I am glad you are part of my family. You are always authentically you, and I respect that. You are a natural comedian. You have no idea how often you lifted my spirits with your humor when I needed it most. You and Glenn would have been a great stand-up team. All joking aside, I love you like a brother.

To my heavenly friends, Bonnie and Kathy, you two may have no idea what an impact you had on me both professionally and personally. I value our long-term friendship, and I think about you both often and with so much love and admiration. I learned so much from both of you. I miss our conversations, but if you listen closely, you will hear me, my treasured friends.

To Dora and Enid, you both hold special places in my heart. You are my two prayer warriors, and God knows I needed you both in my life. Thank you for that. Enid, I thank you for being the light that guided me back to who I really was, and it was no easy task. I also thank you for consistently calling to check on me. Dora (and Tim too), thank you for stopping in to see me and calling to check on me. You are both amazing women that I am grateful to call my friends. I love you both with all my heart.

Laura and Chris, you two, what can I say? Thank you for being there for me. I am grateful to have you in my life. I appreciate both of you for your generosity and selflessness. Your friendship has made a very difficult time in my life so much easier. I will not forget your kindness, and I love you both.

To Joy, Kate, and Andrew, thanks so much for the group texting and the visits. It brightened my day with each text or visit, and I am honored by your thoughtfulness. I enjoy our fun times, and I treasure you for caring. Dianna is fortunate to have such kind friends. I love you all!

Figure 1: Jenn, Dianna and me

Table of Contents

Beauty Is Everything

Beauty, what is it really? For some, maybe it's a person's face, body, or what they wear. A certain personality, an aura that attracts people to them. Or maybe it's nature and the smell of moss in the woods, mountains capped with snow in the wintertime, children playing in the yard, laughing and chasing each other.

It really can be many things. That's what is so intriguing to me about beauty. I love walking in the woods after the rain, the smell reminds me of my home in Maine. Garden shops with plants and flowers everywhere, I want them all. Walking through a museum and seeing history from a different time. Watching people on the street trying to envision where each is going. Catching lightning bugs in the spring after dark and watching them, then letting them go to fly free again.

It's all beautiful, isn't it? How could I choose just one?

PREFACE

My Story

I'm sitting on my patio with a beautiful view of the water just off St. Joseph's Sound on the West Coast of Florida. This is my personal story of strength, resilience, and gratitude put to paper primarily as a tool to assist and encourage others to stay strong and never give up when things get tough. Throughout my life, I have had more than my share of major medical issues. Each medical problem is really a larger story of its own. By consolidating all the events that I can recall into a story format, I am hopeful that they will provide inspiration and strength to many others. I have provided as much detail as I can remember, mostly for my family as a written record. I want them to have something they can refer to when their memories begin to fade or when they need to deal with difficulties in their own lives. I'm certain that I am not the only one who has gone through major life challenges.

I am an amateur writer with a desire to leave some small mark on the world by sharing my personal story. Throughout this book, I will name family members who lived through these events with me, though some passed prior to the writing of this story. This includes, but is not limited to, my parents, Marilyn and Phil, my two amazing and beautiful daughters, Jennifer (Jenn) and Dianna, sister Sue, brother Glenn, Uncle Wayne among others. Those named have lived all or part of our Florida life together. We had a large family, most of which still live in Maine, and they are all incredibly special in my life. My heavenly family includes my great grandmother (Grammie Pierce), my great grandfather (Pop Hunter), and both sets of my grandparents (the Gray and Thomas families). To those named, un-named, and in heaven, I could honestly write a book filled with stories about each of you that left a positive mark on my life. So, please know that when I think of you, I smile.

This story begins in Maine, where I was born, and ends with where I am today. But first, a little about myself.

Figure 2: Five generations of women. Standing left is my Grandmother Thomas, right my mother, Marilyn Gray, seated is my Great Grandmother (Annie Pierce) with me on the right holding Jenn, 1982.

Figure 3: My Grandmother Gray on the left & Grandmother Thomas on the right at a shower for Mom.

INTRODUCTION

What Inspires Me

<u>Renovation & Decorating</u>

My retirement dream had finally become a reality.

I won't lie, the renovation of my new home was a difficult, long-term project. The initial stage was to clean and paint, then I wanted to renovate the entire place. Don't get me wrong, it was a nice place with minimal wear and tear, but I had a vision of what I wanted to do with it. I carefully thought through each room and came up with a plan. For the pieces of the job, there were a few tasks I could do with some family help. My sister, Sue, helped me paint the interior walls of each room. Trust me, I truly detest painting walls, but I loved the finished product. My brother-in-law, Gordon, put up several light fixtures, curtain rods, fans, and spray-painted every cabinet door in the house (kitchen, baths, and bar area). I didn't have much time to get the basics done. I worked late into the night for days to be ready for the big move.

One night, I was in the kitchen cleaning and sanding the cabinet boxes. I had two days before my brother-in-law would be delivering the doors for the cabinets. It was after midnight, and I was sitting on the kitchen floor wiping down all the cabinets so they would be clean, painted, and dry. Suddenly, I heard something fall to the countertop directly behind me. I turned around and saw a glass trinket that had fallen from a shelf and landed right behind me. It should have shattered, but it was fully intact. A wave of chills covered my entire body at the sight. I had been known to cut corners sometimes and not "do the job right the first time." When she was alive, Mom would lecture me about it every single time. It was at this moment I realized she was just letting me know she noticed. So, I got back to work. I cleaned and sanded the cabinet boxes in each room and painted those. I am grateful for all the help I received. I then had a contractor replace countertops in the kitchen, baths, and bar area.

The entire home had the typical Florida tile floors. I had a contractor replace the floors with bamboo. It took more than two months, but it was all worth it. We carefully timed everything to come together well. I guess watching all those reno do-it-yourself shows had been worth the time. Next, the challenge was to furnish and decorate. I went with a modern/French country design. I mixed comfortable, warm fabrics and beautiful antique pieces of natural wood furniture. The style had a touch of the quaintness of French country with a conservative modern flare here and there. I am more than happy with the outcome. It was feeling like home already.

Patio Gardening

I have a beautiful canal view from my patio. The patio gets good direct sun in the late afternoon as the sun sets. Springtime is the perfect time to begin growing orchids. This is something I have dabbled in for a few years, but now I am able to dive deeper into this as a passion. It is a learning experience that I will continue to enjoy for as long as I am able. Some of the orchids I purchased, some I grew and nurtured. Learning to sprout new plants from the previously bloomed stems is my latest success. Next, I am going to try grafting different varieties together. That learning process is in the research stage right now, and it seems to have a higher difficulty level. I'll see how that goes.

Figure 4: Mustache Orchid from my patio garden

I have many plants now growing beautifully in addition to the orchids. I enjoy gardening on a small scale. I have had a Christmas tree growing for almost three years--it's currently two feet tall. The patio is my garden. I love having my morning coffee and breakfast there. Mornings are beautiful with the patio facing west toward the Gulf. It remains shady until mid-afternoon. Living in Florida, especially during the summer, late afternoon is usually when I head inside unless I'm kayaking, at the beach, or at my sister's house for a swim.

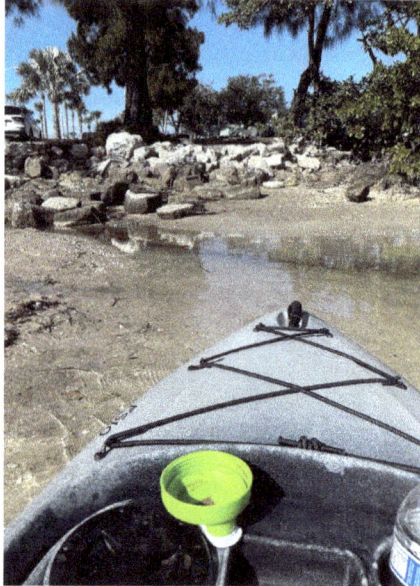

Figure 5: Kayak trip to Sunset Beach in Tarpon Springs, FL

Photography

I also invested time into another hobby I have been interested in for quite a while. When my father-in-law passed away, my sister-in-law, Sheri, gave me his 35mm camera. I signed up for a photography class, so the camera was a blessing. The class was helpful to learn the basics of operating the camera. It was my goal to understand how to use all the settings for improved quality pictures. In each weekly class, we had to learn skills, then take them and apply them by taking photos that demonstrated what we had learned. These were sometimes photographs that were taken during the day and others after dusk. We also learned to take pictures of moving objects, like cars driving down the road, or pictures of the halos from the streetlights that appear when applying certain camera settings. I tend to enjoy capturing unique photos in nature. I get great shots of the sea birds in their natural habitat when I'm kayaking.

Figure 6: Bird Island near the Inter-coastal north of Dunedin Causeway

I have also a special interest in shots of leaves or close-ups of flowers, as well as rainfall when it begins to storm. Learning and applying new skills helps me stay grounded, because it takes my mind off all the other distractions. The instructor required us to save our weekly project pictures to a flash drive and bring it to class each week. The next week the instructor would critique the photos we took. I have included several pictures from my project work. Some of my favorite project pictures include orchids, my two current feline housemates, my patio view, or any still object out in nature that had unique detail. There is an enormous amount of beauty in nature.

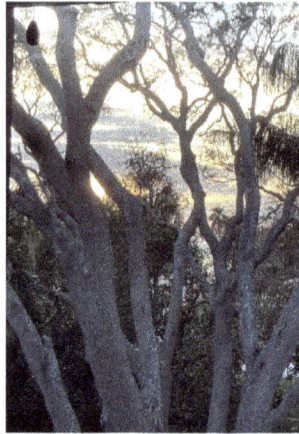

Figure 7: West view from my back patio toward St. Joseph's Sound. This is where I'm inspired to write.

Writing

I always loved writing stories when I was in school—you know the type. The teacher gives you topics to choose from, you write the story. I also dabble in poetry, usually random thoughts that I jot down and wind up turning into a poem. My ultimate passion was truly to write my own story.

But this passion really activated in my sixties. I got out the laptop and began working on my story following a medical event at age sixty-three. This happened after moving into retirement and buying my new home. My goal is to finish and publish my story to date with the ultimate purpose of helping as many people as possible. This may be people who are experiencing a medical situation or other major challenges in life.

Outdoors

You will find throughout my story that I love being outdoors in nature. I enjoy being on the water in any way, and I spend quality time kayaking in St. Joseph's Sound, right off the Central West Coast of Florida. It offers relaxation and a variety of local wildlife to observe, and a great place to apply my limited photography skills.

Figure 8: Honeymoon Island State Park, Dunedin. One of my favorite meditation spots.

I also love to bike ride. Whether it is on the trails in the more wooded parts around Florida or a paved bike path, I enjoy my riding time. We all need to stay moving to keep ourselves healthy, and this is a perfect way to exercise. Florida parks commonly offer bike trails that provide great opportunities to see wildlife in its own habitat.

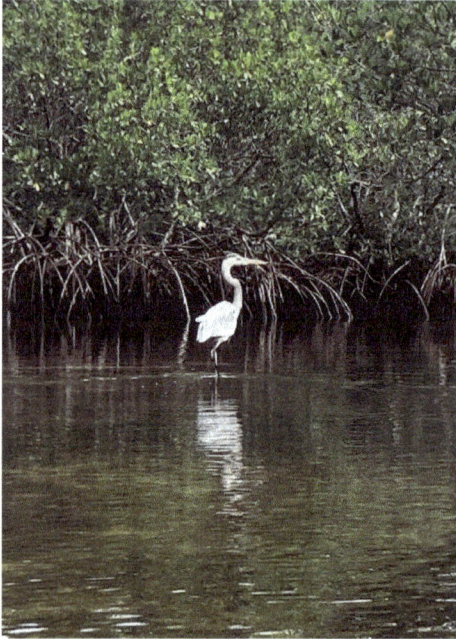

Figure 9: Kayaking at St. Joseph's Sound

CHAPTER 1

The Early Years

I was born in Waterville, Maine, the second of three children. My sister is older, my brother younger. We lived in the small town of Windsor. Growing up in Maine was amazing. It was a vastly different time from today's world. When I was young, kids played outside more, and we did not watch much television or have electronic toys. Television was black and white, and there were only three channels, and they all went off the air by midnight or so. We had to use our imagination and keep ourselves busy. Crime was lower back then. Our parents didn't have to worry about the kind of danger our kids and grandkids have to face today. I know there were many things I was allowed to do that I did not allow my children to do. Our family had a great life there. We had a beautiful home and extended family nearby, most of whom we saw often. My parents built our home after their marriage with some help from family. It looks different today, although the owners who bought the home when we moved away have taken very good care of it. This lifts my heart because my parents worked so hard to build it. Mom was an amazing housekeeper. She was very particular and disciplined to do certain tasks on a schedule in the spring, fall, and into winter. With three small children in the house, her hands were always full, especially since Dad would juggle two or three jobs at times to provide for us. Mom always made a point to have the house in good order when he would get home from work. She taught us to do chores we could help with as we became old enough. We didn't receive an allowance for chores done around the house. It was expected that we would learn how to do certain chores and contribute to the household. If our chores were done, Mom would send us outside to play. I think this may be a direct quote, but the typical comment she would make was "if you can't find something to do, I'll find something for you."

Figure 10: Maine Home

I have so many memories of playing in the woods of Maine, creating makeshift houses there with my sister and brother and playing pretend. It was always a competition to see who would get to be the mom, dad, or child in the make-believe family each time we played. In the summer, during winter when the snow was firm, and in spring when the snow started to melt, my sister and I would follow a small creek that ran back into the woods behind our house to a pond. We loved exploring there, and now I realize just how beautiful it was. Usually, it was my sister and me. My brother was too young at that time to go with us, but we had many outdoor family adventures where we all went on adventures together. I believe this kind of outdoor exploration, or really any activity that forces kids to use their imagination, is what's missing for so many children today. This was the portion of my childhood that helped me develop a lot of creativity. It also created so many beautiful memories.

Figure 11: Me and Sue

I remember one such time when my sister and I wandered out to the pond. It was a long hike for us at that time; we were so young. We pretended to be discoverers. We found many of these pebble-like objects on the ground. We filled our pockets with them and ran back to the house so excited to show Mom. We ran through the door and into the kitchen where Mom had her washer and dryer. We unloaded our pockets with the treasures we found right on the top of her washer. Mom was mortified. They were rabbit droppings. To this day, this story comes up during family conversations, and we still laugh when we talk about this memory.

As we got older, Mom would let my sister take me on the snowmobile out through a path in the woods to the power lines where we could go faster. We only had one neighbor close by, but there were friends and family further down the road that would sometimes meet up with us out at the power lines. I am certain that made Mom a little more comfortable letting us venture off this far by ourselves. It still amazes me that she allowed it at our young age. There were hazards, but we always got excited when we went out.

One time, we were heading out to the power lines. My sister was driving the snowmobile, and I was on the back. There was a lot of snow on the ground. It was deep, soft snow from a very recent storm. We made it all the way down the tree-lined path from the house. As we approached the open space at the powerlines, we next made a turn. The snowmobile tipped to one side burying it in the deep snow. The heavy machine was stuck in a big snow drift. The two of us could not get it upright. So, Sue stayed with the snowmobile, and she designated me to walk back through the wooded path to our house. I will not lie, I was a scaredy-cat when I was young. As I made it out of the woods and into our backyard, I was relieved. A couple of times while walking, I thought I heard something behind me. I would turn around, but nothing was there. So, off I went across the backyard to the steps and into the breezeway to get Mom to come help us put the snowmobile upright. As I turned to look back toward the woods, there was a bobcat standing right at the clearing to our backyard. It seems he took off by the time Mom and I came out of the house to go back to the half-buried snowmobile. Still, it scared me a little, but having Mom with me always made me braver. I had never seen a bobcat before that time. In fact, I never saw another one for as long as we lived there.

Sometimes, we would build tunnels in the snow and pack the sides and top, until they were like ice, and then crawl through them. As I remember it, we were always in the front yard. When we would get a good snowfall, it was the best place to make tunnels. Looking back, Mom most likely made us do it where she could easily keep an eye on us from the large window in the living room. It was a very dangerous thing, but I'm certain Mom watched us more closely than we knew at the time. I remember times when they would report a child that had died because one of these tunnels had caved in and the child suffocated. Snow is heavy and it happens. This is one of the many reasons I'm claustrophobic to this day.

On other days, Sue and I would sled down a small hill next to our house into a boggy area, and then climb back up, and do it over and over again, until we were worn out. There were good sized hills surrounding the bog that we could sled or toboggan down into if the snow was deep and firm enough. Now and then, Sue and I would put my brother, Glenn, on the sled and push him down the hill. The boggy area was the muddiest in the spring when all the snow would melt. Mom would scold us when we came in dirty. Each spring, Mom would take us to shop for new sneakers. I remember having a white pair one year, and I got them dirty playing near the bog. We had been warned not to wear our new sneakers; of course, I did it anyway. I was expecting to get in trouble when we went back to the house, and Mom lectured me. I don't remember what the punishment was, but I knew she wasn't happy with me at all.

I remember playing outside in the backyard one winter. It was very cold, and snow coated the ground. I was playing on the slide attached to our swing set. I remember licking the frost on the slide and getting my tongue stuck on it. Sue had to get Mom, who brought warm water and poured it on the slide to get me unstuck. I laugh now, but that day I was crying. It hurt, but I was more embarrassed than anything else. Once, I saw a comedy where someone did the same thing. I laughed until I cried watching that movie. It would pop into my head on and off for a few days, and I would laugh again. It made me feel like I wasn't the only one to try this ridiculous stunt. I never did it again.

Further into winter, when the ponds in the woods were all frozen solid, Dad and Mom would attach a toboggan to the back of the snowmobile for the three of us to ride behind them. We would go through the path in the woods and out to the ponds. I'm not sure how far the ride was, but it felt like it was long. There would be several families gathering there to cook hot dogs, roast marshmallows, skate, or just ride the snowmobiles around. I loved it when we did this because it was always a great adventure for me. I remember one time when we were out there, I was on the snowmobile behind Dad, and the ice was not quite solid. It didn't break through, but water pooled up on top of the ice. I could see it beneath the belt that propelled the snowmobile forward. I was a little afraid at that moment, but Dad noticed, maneuvered the machine to safety, and we were off the ice in no time at all. I also remember a time when I was on the back end of the toboggan, and we were heading out to meet up with other families. No one wanted to sit in the back, but Mom put Glenn in the middle to keep him sandwiched safely between Sue and me. Suddenly, we hit a bump, and bounced right off the toboggan. It was already dark, so they didn't immediately realize that I had fallen off. I started walking down the path toward them as I cried. I was afraid until I heard them coming back for me. I remember feeling so relieved.

When we got snowstorms that produced heavy snowfall, it would be necessary to shovel off the roof so it would not cave in. My parents would sometimes take us up on the roof with them to keep an eye on us while they shoveled off the snow. We would jump off the roof into the tall snow that had fallen around the house. I remember a year when the snow was so tall, the front door and the garage were blocked by snow that was probably three or four feet high. Mom or Dad opened the big garage door and then shoveled away enough of the snow, so they could get outside. This was necessary in order to clear a path for the outside of the other doors that exited the house. In bad storms, when the people around town with ploughs would be delayed, they had to shovel the entire driveway to access the road. There were snow ploughs that would clear the main roads throughout the town, and our driveway was pretty long. So like many people, my parents would sometimes pay a local person to plough out our driveway. We would get really excited when we had a big snowstorm in the winter because it meant that we might get a day or two off from school. These were fun times as I remember them.

I also had a scary accident during the summer just before I turned four or five. We had an aunt who lived in Augusta, Maine. She was one of our great aunts: Aunt Isabel. Augusta is the capital of Maine and about 13 miles south from where we lived. She had come to our home for a visit. We loved it when she came because she would always bring candy or some sort of treat. Typically, we didn't get much candy unless it was Halloween or during the holidays, so this was always a treat. My Dad had set our tent up in the backyard to air it out for a summer of camping. After storing the folded-up canvas tent all winter, it needed to be cleaned and aired out before we could use it. Camping was one thing we did several times during the summer months. Summer seemed much shorter back then. Camping was a budget-friendly vacation for our family.

This time my aunt came to visit, the adults had settled in the living room, and we were in the backyard playing in the tent. We came in from the backyard and through the breezeway to get to the kitchen. From there, I could see the adults talking in the living room. The plan was for me to ask if we could have more candy. So, I did. I was so gullible and naïve then. My Dad was sitting in his chair by the fireplace and was looking directly at me when I came inside. When I asked if we could have more candy, Dad started to stand up, acting aggravated because we had already asked for more once or twice that day. Dad probably did it so that I'd stop asking. It scared me. I turned to run back out to the yard, but the glass door had closed behind me. My head and right arm both went through the glass door. It was my natural reaction to pull myself back out of the doorframe of the—now broken—glass door.

Of course, everyone then came running into the kitchen frantic from the noise of shattering glass, and I was just standing there looking at my right arm. The fat and tendons were just hanging from it with a pool of blood on the floor. I was in shock. I do remember thinking about how much trouble I was going to be in for breaking the door, but I got no punishment that time. Before I could count to five, Mom had already wrapped a towel around my arm tightly and was carrying me to the car. Dad was right behind us and into the car we went, Dad in the driver's seat, me in the middle, and Mom in the passenger seat. In that moment, Mom saw blood running down my neck. There was another large cut behind my right ear about an inch and a half long. She rushed back into the house for another towel and wrapped it around my neck tightly to slow the bleeding. Dad backed out of the driveway onto the main road and drove in a hurry.

We lived in such a rural area that it was a long drive to the doctor. It was all such a blur. I don't even remember who called the doctor to meet us there. I do remember Dad running a red light at one point, and Mom scolding him. Finally, we were at the hospital. I was put up on the exam table soaked with blood. Mom's shirt was also soaked with my blood. When I think about this now, I realize that we had a particularly good doctor. He had the best bedside manner. He talked with me and helped me calm down, then took a handkerchief from his pocket, folded it over twice, and clipped off the tip of the folds. He put it over my face, so that I could see him through the hole he had clipped in the center.

What he was really doing was keeping me from seeing the huge needles he was going to need to use. He brought the anxiety in the room down with his voice and talked with me throughout the process telling me every single step of what he was doing. This really kept me calm. His name was Dr. Petty. He went right to work, first numbing my arm and neck, before he started stitching. I remember him telling Mom and Dad it was over 100 stitches in total. He also told them that I had come extremely close to suffering serious damage. The cut on my arm was only a quarter inch from severing all the tendons and nerves, and as for my neck, I was only an eighth of an inch from severing my jugular vein. So, this was the first major medical event in my life. Little did I know that this was only the beginning.

Around this time, our family doctor told my parents that I had an unusual and irregular heartbeat. The doctor recommended that they should have me checked out by a specialist. My parents and Grandfather Gray took me to a nearby hospital for tests following the doctor's recommendation. It was a very scary event for me being this young. I was always afraid of hospitals. It was a long day of frightening tests, and at the end of it all, the specialist said they could crack my chest open to attempt to identify the problem and possibly repair whatever the defect was.

Understand that this was the early 60's, they knew very little about these types of irregularities, and technology was not anywhere near as advanced as today. My grandfather told my parents not to do it. "Do *not* let them operate on her," he said. He stated that the surgeons did not know enough to perform such a dangerous operation and that I likely would not make it off the operating table alive. My grandfather was a licensed mortician and funeral director who operated transport and embalming, as well as funeral services. He had solid medical knowledge, so my parents opted not to go the surgery route (thank God). At the time, only an irregular heartbeat was diagnosed by the specialists that day. Our family doctor then encouraged my parents to let me live like any normal child, monitor me, and come back to see him if anything concerned them. And so, my childhood went on without medical incident. Praise God for that. Later as a young adult, I was diagnosed as having MVP, a valve defect.

My siblings and I attended school at Windsor Elementary. Sue was two years ahead of me, and Glenn was three years younger than me. It was a small school with one classroom for each grade level, first through fourth or fifth grade, and multiple classrooms for fifth or sixth through eighth grade. I was a good student but had some struggles with reading in the early grades. I think it was more me being nervous than anything else, worrying that I would have to read in front of class. My teachers made us do this regularly.

I was shy as a child. I preferred to sit in the back of the class and not raise my hand, hoping the teacher would call on others to read aloud. Maybe I was an introvert, although I would have had no idea what that meant at that time. I enjoyed music class and writing stories about what we did over the summer. I loved it when we learned about square dancing or when it was time for lunch or recess. I welcomed getting out of class. I realize now that I didn't hate school or socializing; I just found the structure of school boring. That feeling was true throughout most of my school years except for fifth through eighth grade. Once Glenn was in school, Mom started substitute teaching at our school, as well as some of the schools in the surrounding area. I think she liked getting out of the house and teaching, and she was good at it. She may have wanted to contribute to supporting the household by working. She probably thought it would help take some of the burden off Dad, so he didn't have to work as much. During the summer months, when school was out, Mom would occasionally take care of my cousins. I'm sure this wasn't her favorite job. She managed it well, though, considering some days that meant watching over five or six kids. We had three cousins that were usually there, so with the three of us and three cousins, that had to be tough. She was strict, and she needed to be. She had to resolve arguments frequently when we weren't behaving. We truly tried not to test her. She was a disciplinarian, and we did not like punishment.

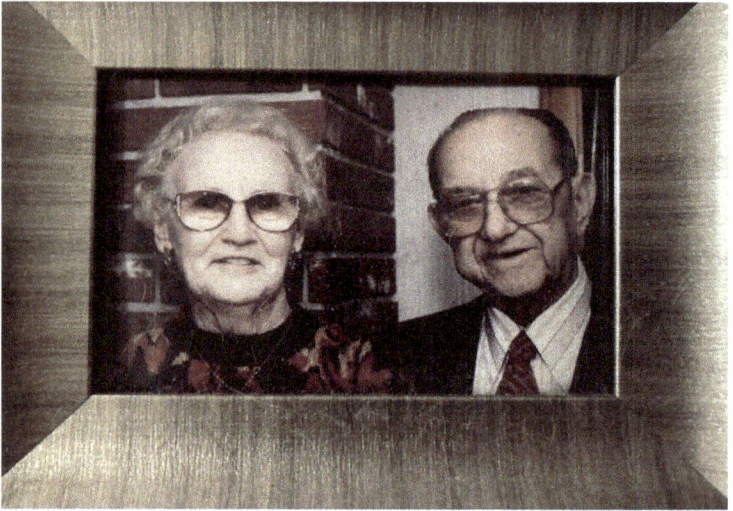

Figure 13: Maternal grandparents, William and Juanita Thomas.

Figure 12: Maternal Grandparents, William and Juanita Thomas's home in Weeks Mills, Maine

Figure 14: Cousins - my Mother's oldest brother, Milford, and wife Carol Thomas's children (Barbara sitting left and Cheryl standing right) and my brother, sister and me

CHAPTER 2

Dad's Visit to Florida

During the late 60's, my paternal grandparents had retired. They had decided to move to Florida and planned on selling their family funeral business in Maine, which was set up in their home. Gramp had a separate room in the hallway that led out toward the barn. It was a laboratory-type room that was set up for embalming. The funerals were held in a separate section of the house that may have been an add-on to their home at some point, specifically made for that purpose.

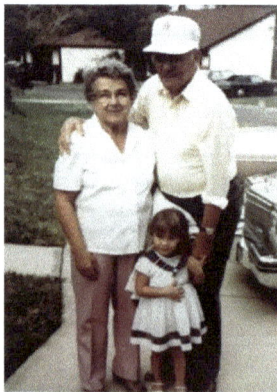

Figure 15: My paternal grandparents and Jenn wearing her dress that Uncle Wayne brought her from So. Korea

My grandmother had been a schoolteacher but later gave up teaching to help Gramp with the funeral business by taking on the tasks of keeping the books, doing hair and makeup for the deceased, and dressing them. It was a small town, and everyone knew everyone there. My grandmother was talented at this part of the business due to knowing most of the people who lived in this area; her skills made the deceased look as if they were just sleeping. This comforted the families who were grieving their loss. This was, however, a difficult job. I am certain that when they needed to perform services for someone they knew very well, or for teens or young children who tragically died, they shed many tears.

Figure 16: William and Sarah Gray Family home and funeral business

My grandparents had visited Florida many times for vacation over the years, and they loved it there. On one visit, when they were getting close to retirement, they contracted to have a home built where they had planned to live after retirement. When the house was ready and the funeral business was sold, Dad and a friend helped move my grandparents to Florida. Dad fell in love with this wonderful place. When he returned to our home in Maine, he told my mother, "We're moving to Florida." They put a For Sale sign in the yard of the home they had built with their own hands. We made the rounds, visiting family and close friends around the state to share the news of our move. Mom began packing what would be going with us and donated the rest of our things to families we knew that needed them. Once the house was sold, Mom and Dad ordered a moving van and filled it for the move. Then, they loaded my sister, brother, and I into our car, and in June of 1969, we were on the road, heading to Florida.

My Dad had no job secured yet, and no plan for where we would live; he just had a dream of what he thought would be a good move for all of us. I remember the first night on the road, we stopped to sleep at a motel. I think this was the first time we swam in a swimming pool, and we could not wait to get done with dinner so that we could go to the pool. The trip was long but exciting. My feeling about the move then remains the same today; this was one of the best decisions Dad ever made, just shy of his decision to marry my mother. He was an extremely lucky man. Mom was a lifelong devoted partner and supporter of whatever would make Dad happy. They had known each other since Mom was thirteen and Dad was fifteen. They were married in June of 1956 and spent the rest of their lives together. Mind you, our maternal grandparents, and a few other relatives who were left behind in Maine, were not so happy about this move being so far away from all of them.

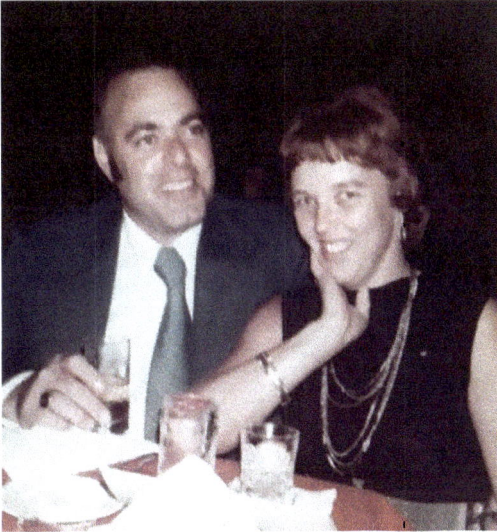

Figure 17: Mom and Dad

Florida was exciting and new. When we first arrived, we stayed with friends my parents knew in St. Petersburg for a bit until they found an efficiency right on Madeira Beach. Since we were staying right on the beach, we played there all day, every day. We kept Mom busy applying aloe on our sunburns. Sunscreen back then was not as protective as it is today. We enjoyed pizza at The Deck which was a great pizza place that was right next door. Mom and Dad would order pizza, and we would eat outside and watch the sunset before my mother would eventually make us shower and go to sleep. On days it would rain, we would watch the waterspouts form and fall away back into the Gulf. The first time we saw the waterspouts, we were all scared to death, and we ran inside for safety. What we did not know was that they rarely come onshore. It was like a dream for me. I remember so much of it, and they are mostly great memories.

Figure 18: Uncle Wayne center, his son Adam on left with wife Mary, his son Aaron on right next to me.

CHAPTER 3

Florida Living

Dad had been job hunting diligently, and one day, he came back to the beach efficiency excited to share that he had been offered a job as a dispatcher with a telephone company in New Port Richey. So, our time at the beach was over. We were sad to leave the beach house, but we had to move and begin school in our new location.

We originally settled in New Port Richey. They bought a home, and my father had started his new job. We adjusted to our new home and schools.

Figure 19: Gray Family in New Port Richey home

We moved from the beach rental to a small two-bedroom, one-bath home. We loved it, even though it was a bit small for all of us. Mom and Dad shared one room, and the three of us had twin beds lined up military style in the other bedroom. When Uncle Wayne made the decision to move to Florida, Dad decided to enclose the screened back porch to create a third bedroom. Mom and Dad took that room, and my uncle and brother took my parents' previous room. Our home was on a side street circle with a recreation center just over a hill, and the local church, library, and city hall were just down the street from our home. The three of us kids had bikes, so we would ride them and explore the area. There was a large empty lot just down the street that was scattered with gopher holes and covered with sandspurs. We would use long sticks to see if we could find a gopher and try to get them out of their holes. We were told to use caution and keep our distance because rattlesnakes use the empty holes to rest and get out of the heat during the late afternoons. I remember having to remind Glenn, who was six at the time, not to get too close. He never listened to me.

Uncle Wayne is Mom's youngest brother. He moved to Florida and moved in with us for a while. It made sense at that time. He was a merchant marine, so he was gone for long periods of time. We looked forward to the times he would be home. He brought a lot of happiness to us as kids. I am sure we drove him crazy fighting for his attention. He was a young adult at the time and would try to get naps in the afternoon sometimes, so he could go out with friends for the evening. That rarely went well. He got a little irritated with us at times when we would wake him up. We really did enjoy his time at home, and it meant a great deal to Mom, who missed her Maine family very much.

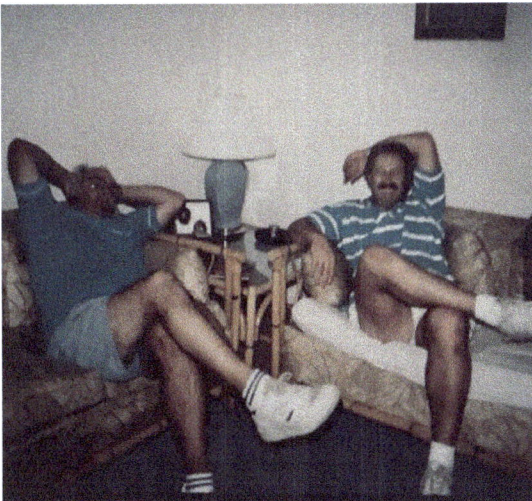

Figure 20: Dad and Uncle Wayne at our Holiday house

After some time had passed, he moved into a duplex rental with a buddy where he stayed for a while. The house was small for six people, so it made sense, but we missed him being there. We did have relatives come down to Florida to visit sometimes. Mom's oldest brother, Milford, his wife, Aunt Carol, and our two cousins, Cheryl and Barbara, would come to see us. We loved it when they visited. They always stayed with us for part of their vacation, and there would be late night card games, which we loved because we could get away with staying up a little later sometimes. Some years, when our family members were down for a visit, we would go to Cypress Gardens, Disney, or Busch Gardens. Mom's other brother, Uncle Barry, and his wife, Aunt Sandra, visited Florida regularly. They loved to play cards with my parents. These were always fun times when anyone would come to visit, and we were always sad when they left.

Figure 21: Our cousin Cheryl on the left, Sue on the right. A trip to Caladesi Island

Sue and I would walk to the library frequently. I must have read every Nancy Drew and Sherlock Holmes book they had there. We would check out as many books as we could from the library, and when we finished them all, we would go back and exchange them for more. We were walking there one day to exchange some books and were barely around the corner from our home when a car pulled up right next to where we were on the sidewalk. The person in the car asked where we were going and if we needed a ride. We declined and the person left. I don't remember if it was a man or woman in the car. Even in the late 60's, there were predators. Today, I realize that Mom must have told us to beware of things like this.

When I was in fifth grade, I had a teacher who was truly amazing. She saw something in me that makes sense now, although it seemed insignificant then. During that time, students were moved to "middle school" which meant sixth through eighth grade. Just before starting sixth grade, this teacher recommended me for an advanced program that was available at that school. She spoke with Mom to get approval for me to enter the program because she felt I was ahead of the work in her lesson plans. She was concerned I would be bored in her class. She must have known this was a situation where boredom could result in a kid going down the wrong path. I'm sure there is some truth to that. So, Mom spoke about it with Dad. I knew nothing about any of this until they spoke with me and told me I would be transferred to this program.

I was scared at the time, and I remember lacking confidence and wondered if I would be able to meet the expectations to be successful in this environment. It was tough for me at first. In this program, advanced students had special schedules. During times slotted for music class and physical education subjects, all the students were together. During times slotted for math, science, history, and English/literature, I was in what they called a "pod" with other advanced students. We were broken into four groups to make smaller study groups. We stayed in our assigned groups until the end of each six-week period. The school administrator would then mix up the students into four new groups. This created opportunities for each of us to learn to work well with others with varying types of knowledge and personalities. I really see the benefit of this process now. The other significant benefit was that we worked on our own a good deal of the time. At the beginning of each six-week period, we were given a package of assignments with instructions. In some assignments, we were required to work with our assigned group. For other assignments, we could work at our own pace, alone, or with one or more people that we chose.

We were required to attend class lectures as scheduled, and testing was scheduled for each of the four subjects. This part of the process was genius in my opinion. I personally learned to be responsible and accountable in a very organic manner. Each of the four teachers had a cubed area where the lectures and tests were done. The teachers were available at all times to help us if we had questions during study-time, which was held in the center area of the four cubed spaces. This area had round tables with four to six seats where we could sit and had research materials there for us to use during our study time. We were encouraged to team up and collaborate with other students.

This program was ahead of its time. I got comfortable, and I began to excel. This was the environment where I spent the majority of my day. I believe now that I learned so much, due to this environment, about being responsible for myself, being accountable for my actions, learning to research topics, and so much more. It seems obvious now, but it was a challenge for me then. I can now say I conquered many fears and grew my confidence quite a bit by being in that program. Later in my career, I would be labeled the "Research Queen" by a vice president I worked with because of what I learned from working in this environment. I am honored to have been given that label. I am still compelled to research everything I get involved in whether it is job-related or just a topic of interest.

CHAPTER 4

Living in Dunedin

In the middle of my eighth-grade year, Dad was promoted to a management position at the telephone company. This prompted a move for the family to Dunedin, so Dad's commute would be less time-consuming. Dunedin was, and still is, a quaint town. Today, Dunedin is a unique mix of people and fun things to do. Tourists are many, and the town now has dozens of restaurants and shops that draw in the crowds. However, this move was difficult for my sister, who was entering her junior year in high school, was involved in cheerleading, and had a solid friend group she had to leave. I remember this being a terrible time for her to make such a big change. For me, it felt like just another move, although I missed the school program I had been in prior to the move to Dunedin. However, the move was a good opportunity for our family, overall. We were so excited about the new Dunedin home. Glenn had almost always had his own room, but it was the first time Sue and I had our own bedrooms. I know it is pretty common today for a lot of kids, but it was a big plus for Sue and me at that time. So, we all adjusted in our own way. It was a much larger home, so we had space for family who came to visit.

Figure 22: My brother, the jokester, Glenn

The new Dunedin home was on an inside corner lot with the driveway making up most of the front yard. Being an inside corner lot, it was shaped like a slice of pie with the narrow part of the pie being the driveway and getting wider as the property went toward the lake. It was a large backyard on Lake Diane with Gardenia bushes across the backside of a good portion of the house where my sister, brother, and my bedrooms were, and tall hedges of ligustrum stretched down each side of the driveway, past the house, all the way down to the lake. It was a beautiful property. The bedrooms for my brother, sister, and I had windows that opened out to the row of Gardenia bushes. It always smelled amazing when they bloomed. Mom, who always stuck to a budget, would have the windows open as much as possible. This was when I realized I was allergic to Gardenias. I was miserable until it was hot enough for the windows to be closed and the air conditioning to be turned on for the summer.

With the large backyard, Mom and Dad decided to buy a riding lawn mower. It was my brother's job to mow the yard. I remember my brother getting too close to the edge of the lake one time, and the lawn mower slipped down almost all the way into the lake. I don't remember if there was damage to the new lawnmower. Mom was always planting flowers, pulling weeds, or trimming the enormous hedges. On the hedge trimming days, when we were home, we would be asked to help bag up all the hedge trimmings and pile them out front to be picked up. Mom worked in the yard constantly, and it was a huge task. This home also had a swimming pool. We loved that and felt very grateful at the time. Pools are common now but not so much back then. Mom kept that pool sparkling, and she had the best tan during those years.

It was during this period that my parents and Uncle Wayne had decided to buy a boat together. We weren't wealthy, but my parents were savers. They found a great deal on a 28-foot Chris Craft cabin cruiser. It was a real stretch for them, and it would need a good amount of work. They made the purchase and decided to keep the name on the boat. It was called the "TriPaddlin." Dad and Uncle Wayne were very skilled with mechanical things, so they had some work to do on the engines; the boat also needed repairs and painting. The depth/fish finder was included on the boat, but this required figuring out how it worked. I remember them saying how expensive it was doing all the work needed to get the boat in working order, but they would save up money and do one thing at a time until it was ready for its maiden voyage. The repairs eventually got done, and the boat was ready for family adventures. This was a very exciting time for me. These were the years when I fell in love with the ocean. We would spend vacations, holidays, and long weekends on the water. There were other families that my parents connected with at the marina where we housed the boat, and we all became friends. These connections formed bonds to the point that trips were sometimes planned together.

The owner of the marina was a kind man. His name was Vin Barkley. He had a boat launch and sold gas and bait for fishing, along with candy, chips, and drinks for patrons; all of which kept him very busy. Sometimes Sue or I would work the counter for him when he was busy doing other things. It kept me distracted when my parents were getting the boat ready to go out or when they were cleaning it up to head home. Vin also had a shrimp boat. He would go out weekly to catch shrimp to use as live bait that he also sold at the marina to patrons.

Figure 23: On the shrimp boat with Mom and Vin Barkley

Mom and I got interested enough in how that worked and decided to accept an invitation from Vin to go out with him sometime to see how it was done. This was so exciting. I fell in love with shrimping, and Mom and I went almost every Tuesday if we could. Of course, when you use shrimp nets, you find all other kinds of treasures when you pull them in to collect the shrimp. We always made sure to throw those treasures back to the ocean so as not to impact the environment. Of those treasures, I remember rays, blowfish, ballyhoo, cowfish, and so many more. At that time, the other benefit to helping him collect shrimp was that we could save the largest shrimp to cook and eat them when we'd get back to the marina.

It was during these late-night shrimp feasts that Vin showed us his home. He lived just a short walk directly across the street from the marina. He had a passion for oil painting. Vin's wife had previously passed away, so I think we were good company for him at that time in his life. He saw the curiosity in me for painting and offered to give me lessons.

He taught me how to use oil paints, how to use different brushes for various techniques, and how to use knives for adding texture and showing depth.

I thoroughly enjoyed these times. I still love to paint. I am definitely not a pro at it, but I do enjoy it from time to time. Sometimes when I reflect on this, I'm surprised I didn't end up becoming an artist for a living. Too young at that time, I guess. I was sixteen and going through my teen years, but it was a joy in my life that I will never forget. I did run into Vin long after that. I was married by then and at a local grocery store. Vin was leaving the store when my husband and I were entering the store to shop. We had a nice chat. He told me he had remarried and sold the marina. I was so happy for him. He was late in life, and no one deserved to find love more than him. He was someone in my life that was giving; he expected nothing in return and was so kind to share his knowledge. I am certain he's an angel by now, and he probably watches over me to this day. He was humble and a great example for me when I was at an impressionable age.

During my high school years, I was a rebel. I was still a good student, but I challenged everything with my parents. I did not respond well to rules, and this got me grounded so many times. I remember one time I was grounded. I'm not sure which event caused it since there were so many. More than likely, I didn't get home by curfew or was talking back to Mom. This wasn't unusual for me. By this time, my uncle had moved into the Dunedin house with us and, fortunately, was not out on a ship working. He talked to Mom and convinced her to let me go with him down to Clearwater Beach where we played frisbee for a while before heading back home. I think we may have stopped for ice cream too. When Mom and I were together, it was a recipe for disaster that would get me grounded even longer sometimes. She was trying to teach me a lesson, and I was rebelling.

My uncle probably realized that and wanted to give Mom a break by getting me out of the house for a little while. I appreciated that, and I think Mom probably did too. I am sure my uncle doesn't realize how much of a positive influence he had on me. When he would be out on a ship, I would sit in his room and play his albums on the record player. I loved Don McLean's *American Pie* album and Janis Joplin's "Me and Bobby McGee." His influence impacted my future in a very positive way.

Figure 24: My high school days

In high school, I continued to get good grades. Well, I did struggle a little with my Algebra grades. The rest of the schoolwork came easy to me even though some of it bored me terribly. I got involved in cheerleading, and Sue and I joined a city softball league while Glenn played baseball during elementary school before eventually playing football for Dunedin High School. We all enjoyed sports. When each of us turned sixteen and got our licenses, Dad and Mom bought us our first cars; used, of course, and with the condition that we had jobs. That was when my work life began. We were required to pay them back for our cars, one of many lessons of life they taught us: nothing is free. My first car was a 1966 white Ford Mustang with a 289 engine and custom two-tone leather pony interior. My dad had a friend who owned a dealership and got good deals for all of us. The car even had air conditioning, which wasn't common like it is now. I think my Mustang cost $800 at the time. I loved this car.

Figure 25: DHS Cheerleading

I graduated high school when I was seventeen, and when I turned eighteen, I ventured out on my own. I did not like that I had to be home by 11 p.m. on nights that I went out with friends. Dad said that was "too bad" and that the only other option was for me to move out. So, I moved out. It was not a pleasant conversation. But it was just what I needed in order to grow up a bit.

Figure 26: My high school graduation

My first home after moving out was a friend's duplex. It was a two-bedroom and one-bath unit, and it was tight. I shared a bedroom with a girlfriend and in the other bedroom was a woman and her daughter. I later moved to a smaller apartment of my own. During this time, I met the man who would become my husband, and after a time we decided to get married. This knocked that rebel in me down a notch or two because I had bills to pay and not as much time or money to play.

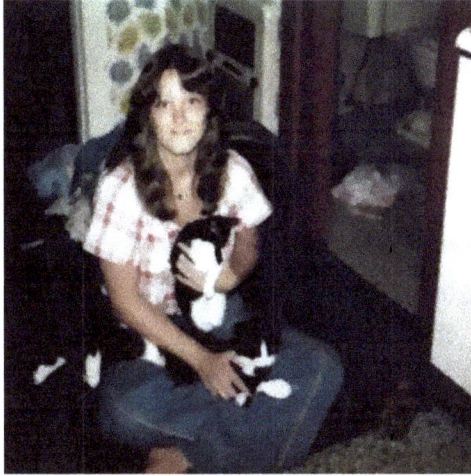

Figure 27: First apartment with my cat, Sylvan

When I reflect on this period of my life, I know I definitely did not make my teenage years easy for my parents. Years after I moved out, Dad and I would sit on his front porch and talk when I visited him and Mom. By that time, Mom had told me that Dad felt regret for forcing me to move out. He wished he had handled it differently. One evening, I was on the porch talking with Dad. I made a point to tell him how much I appreciated that he gave me the choice to live by his rules or move out. I told him it was the best lesson for me at that time. I told him that because I moved out, I quickly had to begin being more responsible, paying bills, and managing a budget. In other words, it forced me to grow up.

Until years later, there were no further conversations with my parents about my teen years that I remember. When I was in my 50's, I made a phone call one night to Mom and Dad. I was inspired to do this because of a friend of mine who had shared something personal with me. It was the last time we talked about my teen years. I wanted them to know that I was very appreciative of all the things they taught me and how sorry I was for being so difficult as a teen. We talked for a long time that night. We all sobbed a little on that call, but I felt compelled to tell them how I realized all the things they did right and how much I appreciated them for the foundation they had given me growing up. Dad was so emotional he had to get off the phone after a little while.

Today, I am so thankful I made that call while they were both still alive. I truly believe God provided me with the best parents. They were tough, but we were raised the right way. None of us are perfect parents, but we do the best we can with what we know. My parents taught us to be hard workers, to be self-sufficient, to learn how to take care of the things we had, and to always respect ourselves and others.

I have to say, although I believe life is made up of ups and downs, my memories are overwhelmingly amazing. I'm not sure if my parents planned to raise us in a certain way or if it just came naturally to them. They used situations or events, some good and others not as much, to teach us lessons. I see that very clearly now. I feel very fortunate to have had a loving home and great parents who may have been strict but taught my sister, brother, and I to be responsible adults who had the ability to make it on our own and contribute to society. I thank God for them all the time. Everyone should be so fortunate.

Figure 28: Mom and Dad, they loved dancing.

CHAPTER 5

Juggling Career and Family

As a teen, I worked part-time during high school waitressing in the dining room of a local nursing home. This had to change when I was on my own, so I decided to work at a real estate office where I maintained escrow accounts on rentals for the owner, typed listings and real estate contracts for home purchases for the agents who worked there, along with other, more basic, clerical tasks. This job was valuable in teaching me to manage my expenses better and to learn about the real estate field. Still, in the end, I knew it was not what I wanted long term.

I interviewed for and accepted a job as an executive secretary for a citrus manufacturer in Safety Harbor, Florida. I was fortunate to participate in two acquisitions during my employment there. This would become valuable later in my career. I learned about business processes, reporting, employee relations, recruitment, and so much more over the course of 23 years, with my final position being HR

Manager. During my employment there, I was able to begin to travel outside the U.S., making several trips to Europe during the second acquisition. This was nothing short of an amazing experience.

Even with a busy work schedule, life never paused for me when it came to personal events. It was in September of 1979 that I married my husband. We took a week off from work for our honeymoon because that was what we could afford to do at this time in life. We drove south toward the Florida Keys. Unfortunately, there was a hurricane approaching, so we stayed in Venice for a couple of days and had to return home. We later had two daughters, Jenn and Dianna, respectively, who were almost five years apart in age. I worked until six weeks before Jenn was born and almost up to my due date with Dianna. I had to return to work six weeks after each of them were born. Leaving them with their babysitters and going back to work was the hardest thing to do. I didn't focus much on work during the first week or two back at work each time. My mind was consumed with how they were doing. They have both been huge blessings in my life, and although my marriage did not survive, I am thankful that it gave me two incredible children and would not change that. I went forward and have lived a single life ever since that period.

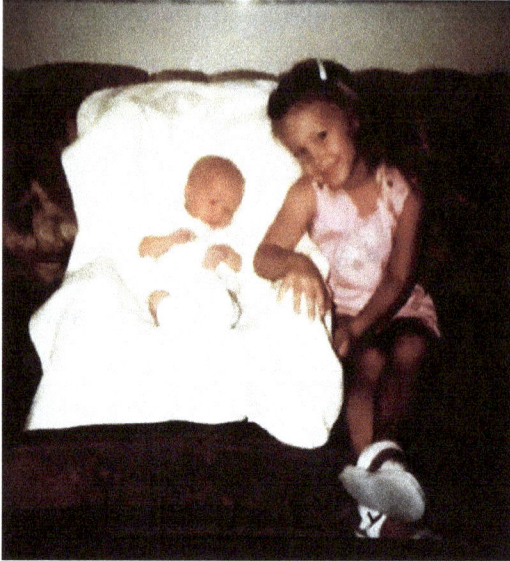

Figure 29: Jenn with little sister Dianna

Jenn started pre-school when she was four. Initially, she was cared for by my mother-in-law, who loved babysitting Jenn. I am forever grateful to her in many ways, but her love for my children is beyond words. When my mother-in-law no longer babysat, one of my very best friends took care of Jenn in her home. She had a son Jenn's age and a daughter who was already in school. She was amazing with her own kids, and Jenn loved going to her house. She was a lifesaver to me when Jenn was a baby since I had to work. I could not have left her with just anyone. Jenn also had issues with biting during this time. There were several times when she was cutting teeth where she had some gentle discipline for this. The habit was quickly nipped in the bud. This, more importantly, ensured that the biting would not happen when Jenn made the transition to school.

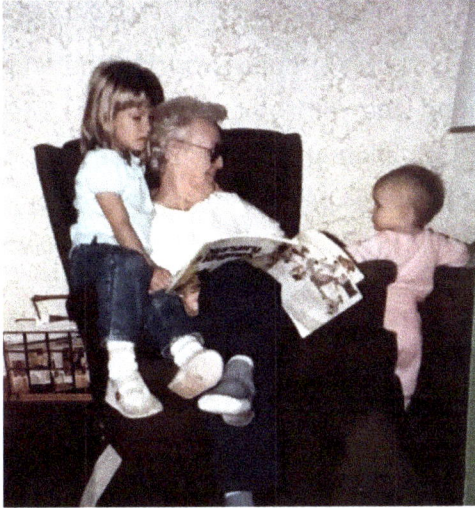

Figure 30: Jenn and Dianna with my maternal Grandmother, Juanita Thomas at their Weeks Mills, Maine home

The school Jenn first attended was small and privately owned by a lovely British couple. Jenn did well there and learned basic Spanish at four years old. They were very progressive at this school. I was pregnant with Dianna at this point. I had to do some juggling here because we had a unique situation of living a long way from where we worked, and we only had one car. Our commute at the time was difficult because we would drop the girls' dad first at his job, and then I would drop Jenn at school and drive to work. The evenings were equally difficult in getting home. Sometimes we would eat with my mother and father-in-law and then drive home by 8 p.m. or so. I would get everything ready for the next day while Jenn's dad got her in the bath and ready for bed. In 1984, I enrolled Jenn in a new school. It was also privately owned by a very nice couple. Jenn would be in the pre-k class. They had a great academic lesson plan. They even taught the kids to do basic gardening. They grew vegetables on the playground property and taught the kids about planting and nurturing the garden. They had very creative and stimulating activities for the kids, which made me very happy, especially when Jenn came home telling me all about it. Jenn graduated from kindergarten at this school when she was six.

By this time, Dianna had been born, and she went to the home of a woman who was licensed to take care of infants. She had an opening for an infant at the time, and I had to return to work. She was a lovely woman, and this worked out very well until she, unfortunately, had a major health situation. I had to find a new sitter for Dianna right away because I only had two weeks' notice, and screening and meeting with potential sitters was a time-consuming process. I felt like I was taking too much time off work to get this done, but I found someone within a week, thank God. I was fortunate to have a very understanding boss. The new babysitter seemed very nice, and her home was close to where I worked. Unfortunately, this one didn't work out so well. Long story short, her license had expired, and there were other issues preventing her from working, so I had to find Dianna yet another sitter and take more time off. I did find a great woman on the second interview who watched Dianna from then until she was out of diapers and ready to be enrolled at the same school where Jenn had been attending. Dianna was two years old by this time, and there was an opening. So, Dianna was with the toddlers, and Jenn was in kindergarten.

When Jenn began first grade, I moved the girls to a small, private Christian school. It was a good place for them and offered a standard class environment with one class for each grade, and it kept my commute about the same. This was also a great opportunity for the girls to be exposed to their faith, and this was important to me. The girls both did very well there. Dianna graduated from kindergarten here, and they stayed at this school until we moved to Lakeland in 1994.

Figure 31: At our Lakeland home. Dove/Mauger side of the family, cousins Kate & Liz Mauger pictured with Jenn & Dianna.

I was learning a lot of new things about the citrus business at this point in my career. I held positions in reception and was an executive secretary to the general manager. I covered as backup to the customer service manager and to the sampling department, and I wrote procedures. I was asked to take over developing an Affirmative Action Plan for the company. This was the first human resources task I was given. The company was a government contractor, so they were required to follow our corporate programs through a formal Affirmative Action Plan. I loved this assignment and delivered their first plan. We had grown as a company, and it was time that they needed a full-time HR person on site. It was then that they made me the HR Manager. I was excited to go down this career path. I had the opportunity to develop HR policy and procedures, participate in larger projects like moving our business from Safety Harbor to Lakeland, FL, and develop basic safety processes with a newly hired Safety Manager.

The citrus manufacturing job had included us acquiring the newer facility in Lakeland. The owners decided to move the business and some employees to the new facility. The Safety Harbor facility was then sold, and we moved the last of the employees to Lakeland. The timing was good because Safety Harbor was growing and the plant distilled citrus oil, which, although not toxic at all, bothered many of the surrounding residents. This was a smart move for the company and allowed for significant business growth.

During this period, I began traveling to Europe. Our sister company in England had just opened a state-of-the-art manufacturing plant, and we were to collaborate with them to develop our plant safety policy and recruitment processes. It was just after my 23-year anniversary with the company that I experienced my first layoff. The company was restructuring to a centralized HR model and did not require my position in their new model. The job market was slow at this time, and it took me seven months to find a new job. It was also the first time I recognized God having a hand in my career, but not the last. I did not realize at the time the value of all I had learned through my experience with this company.

Figure 32: Day trip to Stonehenge during a trip to England.

I am forever grateful for my manager at this company. He saw my potential when he hired me and taught me so much about business, strategy, planning, and reporting. Good leaders are difficult to find, and he always took the time to provide the reasoning behind each report and how each piece of data would impact the bottom-line numbers. His method of training taught me a great deal, all of which I needed to understand to deliver effective reporting to corporate. These skills proved to be critical in each job I worked after this one. Now, I know that I was meant to leave when I did. I had, after all, learned the value of a human resources role in understanding and supporting business and processes. I knew at this point that understanding these important characteristics of the job could prove the importance and business value of HR in any company. I applied this knowledge-building exercise each time I changed jobs after this point in my career. I was devastated at the time of my layoff, but now, I see it as God's hand guiding me to a new challenge. Clearly, He was in charge of my career development and wanted me to learn something new and different from the path I had been on.

When we moved into our new Lakeland home, Jenn went into middle school, and Dianna went into third grade. Initially, I enrolled them both in public school, but this wasn't working. Within a year of moving to Lakeland, I moved them both to another small, private Christian school nearby. The girls both graduated from high school there. The school gave them a great education due to the small size of the classes, the dedicated teaching staff, and the curriculum.

Figure 33: Jenn's high school graduation

They also had a girls' volleyball team. Both Jenn and Dianna played volleyball during their high school years. I went to most of their games, and I was so grateful they had this opportunity at such a small school. They still maintain friendships with some of their classmates from there. They built strong bonds with them, which ventured outside of their time as students together. It is my belief that this is one of many benefits of going to a smaller school. The teachers also were able to dedicate the time necessary to focus on each student and teach them the importance of faith.

Unfortunately, this was when my layoff from the citrus manufacturer occurred. Had Dianna been out of high school, I would have made the move from Lakeland back to Pinellas County, but she was going into her senior year, and I just didn't want to move her at this point in time. I remembered how difficult it had been for my sister when we had to move when she was going into her junior year of high school. I wanted Dianna to graduate with her friends. So, I took a temporary position for a year or so, doing compensation work for a Lakeland airbag inflator manufacturer. Although I didn't see the value of the temporary job at the time, it would prove to be a key factor to the next opportunity of my career, as this position added automotive industry experience to my resume. I was also able to work on a portion of their Six Sigma implementation project that their engineers were rolling out. This would give me valuable knowledge that I would later use for the progression of my career.

Being in Lakeland had provided me with so much valuable experience, but my most treasured experience there was finding my way back to my faith. My family was not big on formal church affiliation, but we were raised with Christian values. We went to Sunday School and attended summer Bible School classes at the local Baptist church in Maine. My sister and I even sang in the choir at a local Methodist Church in Florida. I attended multiple denominations of churches with different friends throughout my younger years. I was married in the Lutheran church, and myself and my daughters were all baptized in this same church. But as an adult, I drifted away from attending, although I still raised my girls with the same values I was taught. I met some of my very best friends in Lakeland.

Figure 34: Lakeland house with The Dove, Mauger, & Acker family visit for Jenn's birthday

Figure 35: Sister, Sue - Sushi for dinner?

One friend in particular was another blessing in my life. She was one of those friends you can go for long periods of time without seeing or talking with, and when you do reconnect, you pick right up where you left off. She was the person that led me back to my faith. Trust me, she more than earned her friend status. She finally got me to attend a small group meeting with her, and that was all it took. I started looking forward to the small group meetings held weekly, where people met to support each other and learn methods to live life as Christians. I also looked forward to the weekly services. It's been a long time since I moved back to Pinellas

County, but I still have not found a church where I felt the genuine presence of God so clearly and consistently. To all my old friends who I haven't seen in a while, all of you fed my soul. The entire experience changed my life for the better. I am forever grateful for this.

The time came when the temporary position came to an end. Moving to a communications media company was my next challenge. The temporary job had allowed me to meet and work with a wonderful and intelligent woman who was both the compensation director and my direct manager. Meeting her was truly a blessing in my life. I learned so much from her and consider her a friend to this day. She recommended me for an interview with this Largo area media company. This company was building a team to work on a confidential project that would turn into an incredible opportunity for me. This was also the opportunity that brought me back to Pinellas County and near the beaches where I longed to be. The project was the best challenge of my entire career. I met and worked with great people, and the project turned out very successful. It gave me an opportunity to apply the Lean Manufacturing principles for which I had previously been certified. It was also where my previous Six Sigma experience could be useful. We applied these principles when designing the new facility and the jobs employees would be doing. This opportunity added media communications industry experience to my resume and included some new and different manufacturing processes for the printing industry's product line. I worked there for a little over seven years, but, unfortunately, this job would become my second layoff. I was an HR Director at that time, and we also had a Compensation Director. The parent company forced a downsizing, and one of us had to go. I was not happy to leave this opportunity, but things have a way of working out.

Frankly, my intuition told me it was happening even before I received the formal news, but I didn't want to leave that job. However, when I got home that day and was a bit calmer, I could see that it was God working in my life once more. Although I now had to search for a new opportunity, I was confident it wouldn't take long to secure a new position.

Within two weeks of my layoff, I was offered a position for a company who designed and built large scale water treatment equipment for large water treatment plants. Once designed and built, the equipment would later be installed with the help of our field services team at locations all over the world.

I welcomed this opportunity. I was now an HR leader for a global manufacturer. They were based in Tampa, Florida. I had just bought a new home in Clearwater, and so for the first couple of years, I commuted to Tampa. Eventually, I temporarily moved to Tampa to minimize my commute. It was not a bad drive in the mornings, but the rush hour traffic in the evenings was a challenge. My home was vacant, so this happened to be a blessing because my youngest, Dianna, lived there during my absence until she bought her first home.

Figure 36: Dianna and Roger wedding 12/2022

Figure 37: Dianna, Roger and me.

During this time in my life, I was always busy with my career. I had been divorced, had two grown daughters who were, and still are, the most important priority of my life. Overall, I felt grateful that God brought me back to my desired location. I had missed being near my parents, extended family, the beaches, and the activities available there. I am so glad it all happened the way it did because it was not long after the move back to Clearwater that we lost Dad, and a couple of years later, Mom passed. I was grateful to be with each of them in their final moments.

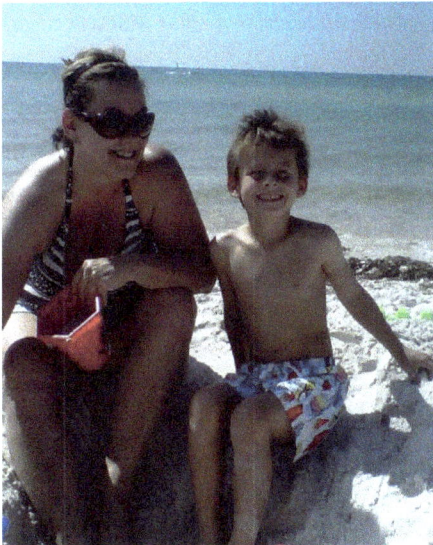

Figure 38: Taking my Grandson to the beach. Honeymoon Island State Park.

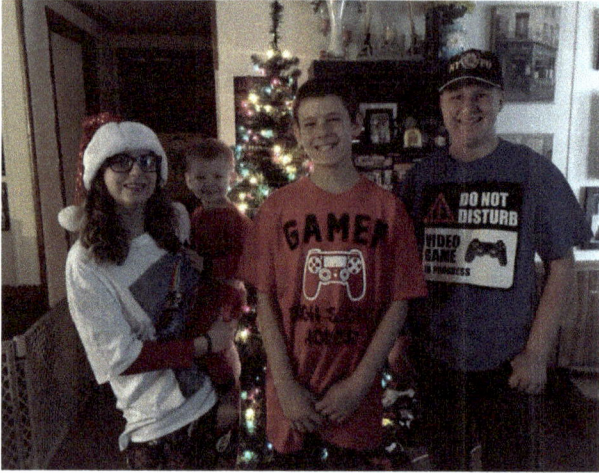

Figure 39: Grandchildren - Jenn & Brian's children

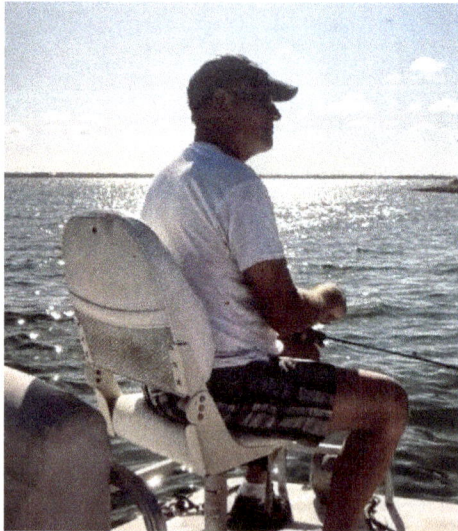

Figure 40: Brother in Law, Gordon - a fishing trip with friends.

Figure 41: Jenn and Brian wedding

Figure 42: Jenn's wedding day. Getting ready!

Figure 43: Dianna getting ready for her big day with Irelynn

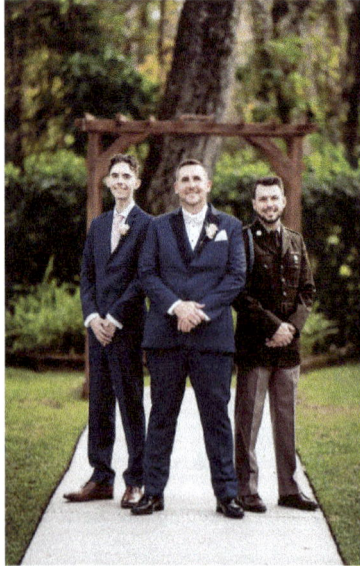

Figure 44: Roger and his sons, Ryder left, Roger center, Tanner right

CHAPTER 6

Medical Challenges

When it rains, it pours, right? Early one morning in 2010, I had showered and was getting ready for just another day at work. I stood in front of the mirror and was shocked to see many very large, bruise-like splotches all over my abdomen. They did not hurt at all, which left me completely clueless about what was going on. I finished getting ready and went to work with the plan to call the doctor as soon as their office was open. When I spoke with the doctor and shared what I had seen, he instructed me to come in right away. So off I headed to the doctor's office. Long story short, the doctor immediately sent me to the hematologist on staff for bloodwork. After ruling out all known diseases and illnesses, I was diagnosed with immune thrombocytopenia (ITP). This is a rare autoimmune blood disorder that causes a low platelet count. This means that the body's blood doesn't clot properly, which can lead to low platelet counts and increased bleeding.

ITP is a condition that I was born with. Some people with this condition live their whole lives without ever knowing they have it. It frequently shows up when there is severe trauma to the body due to bacterial infection that triggers symptoms like mine. It can remain dormant for years until something triggers it. I had been experiencing a stubborn infection, and unfortunately, the antibiotics I had been taking were not clearing it up. Since this was my only issue, my doctor referred me to a urologist for another round of crazy tests, to see if I had an underlying infection that could be the cause. As all less invasive testing showed nothing, they then sent me for a scan of my kidneys. Low and behold, there it was. A golf ball-sized kidney stone in my left kidney. The kidney was seriously inflamed and full of infection. The tests showed that my kidney was functioning only around 20%. This of course forced the other kidney to work that much harder, which could do additional damage. Now, I was scared.

The urologist sent me to another specialist who inserted a stent into the kidney. They indicated this may allow the infection to clear up. I was put on strong antibiotics to help my body kill the infection. After a few months, they checked my kidney function again. I was hoping that they could surgically remove the stone from the kidney. Unfortunately, that next kidney function test showed only minor improvement. The specialist indicated I could wait a few more months to see if it improved any further. He gave me very little hope that it would be possible to see the improvement needed at this point. So, this was my first major surgery. They removed my left kidney using a laparoscope.

I was in the hospital for three days. From the moment I came home from surgery, I had a lot of pain. I expected pain, but even with medicine, it was unbearable. I contacted the doctor. This was feeling like an unusually difficult recovery. The doctor did not take my complaints seriously when I told him I didn't feel like I was healing properly. I called multiple times complaining about severe pain and my inability to move around without serious discomfort. He finally gave in, and I went back for him to examine my wound. Much to his surprise (but not mine), my abdomen was completely herniated. The doctor referred me to a general surgeon to repair my abdomen. Although he was apologetic, I was angry. Why did he not listen to me when I had been calling and telling him how painful it was, and that I was sure something was wrong? Despite my anger, I maintained my composure and took his referral to a surgeon who could repair my abdomen.

I then met with the recommended general surgeon who did a thorough exam. She was very sympathetic. She ordered a new scan to prepare for the surgical repair. Not only was she shocked I was walking around with this herniation, but she also found a very large stone in my gallbladder that only added to her disbelief. She sat with me and shared her scan side-by-side with the scan the previous surgeon had taken prior to my kidney removal. This revealed that the stone had been there all along. Again, I was angry with the medical malpractice I had faced. Why did they not see this with all the scans they had done prior to using the laparoscope? They could have removed both my kidney and gallbladder with one surgery and perhaps avoided this herniation all together.

Now, the more mature version of myself knows I should have acted sooner. At the time, however, I did not. I was raised to believe that doctors were experts, and that suing was wrong because it raised the cost of healthcare. I was so naive, so tired, and had been living in so much pain. I just wanted to heal. So, the surgery was scheduled to remove my gallbladder and reconstruct my abdomen. This surgeon was very good, and within five days, I was home and feeling much better. I worked from home for a couple of weeks, and then I went back to the office part-time. I wasn't yet at 100%, but I took it slow and worked as many hours as I could. I was fortunate to have a very supportive CEO who didn't want me to overdo it. I was able to work from the hospital and then a couple of weeks at home, thanks to his flexibility.

This was an unusually difficult time for our family. Besides my issues with surgery and trying to recover, Jenn was pregnant with twin girls and had just found out that the pregnancy was at risk. She already had a son, and we were looking forward to welcoming twin girls. However, Jenn had gotten some alarming news. Her twins were diagnosed with TTTS (Twin to Twin Transfusion Syndrome). She and her husband would need to fly to Texas right away to have a procedure to correct the problem. There was not much time. She was quickly approaching her due date. I could not go to be with her since I had just had major surgery. Sadly, she went into labor shortly following the procedure, and the twins were born but did not survive.

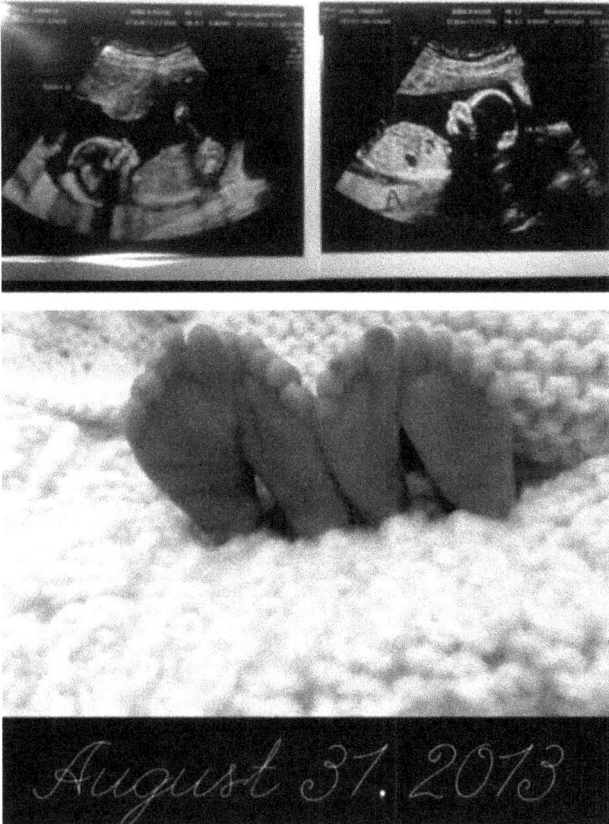

Figure 45: Jenn and Brian's twins, Andrea and Gail

We were all heartbroken, and this was devastating for Jenn and her husband. However, they later had a son, and I am grateful to have two grandsons who are loved very much, as well as two angel granddaughters who we will always treasure and keep alive in our hearts.

Figure 46: Grandsons

Figure 47: Jenn's wedding day

CHAPTER 7

Heart Stopping Trip to China and Egypt

The next several years at work were filled with multiple layoffs due to business results, as well as planning and executing an office move just a couple of blocks away to better fit the business' needs. By this time, we were a smaller company. When I was hired, we had about one hundred employees, and after the first layoffs, we were down to eighty employees. Our company was Korean-owned, so I made two trips to South Korea during this time. This, along with all the other HR tasks like benefits, recruitment, employee relations, pay, systems changes, and so on, made time fly.

Figure 48: Walking tour in South Korea

Soon after the move, I had an important business trip. Our business had now been acquired by a Chinese company and was being restructured. I was invited to go to China and Egypt for meetings. First, for a finance meeting in China, then I went to Egypt, via Thailand, for a major presentation to the new owners of our company. I was the global HR leader tasked to share thoughts and strategies for uniting our company. This meeting included all the senior leaders from each location.

While in China, myself and my co-worker, (who represented the business's finance group), were dinner guests of the Chinese owner, along with several Chinese government dignitaries. We had a multi-course adventure of many foods I had never dreamed of eating. The Chinese food we eat in the U.S. is nothing like authentic Chinese food.

Unfortunately, it was simply not my preferred kind of food. Still, it was an experience to meet all the guests, and we ate and drank for hours (I minimized my alcohol intake due to the guest list).

At the end of the dinner, my co-worker and I made our way to our rooms for the night. I was simultaneously exhausted and energized. It was a huge day. I enjoyed the beautiful hotel room they had gifted me with, and I stood in a lavish shower for an hour, decompressing and analyzing the events of the evening. I fell onto my bed fully expecting to pass out immediately. The opposite happened. Suddenly, I had severe pressure in my chest, and my heart was palpitating furiously. I shifted back and forth on the bed, got up, walked around, then took a blood pressure pill under the assumption it was such a big day that my blood pressure must be high. About a half hour later, the symptoms subsided slowly, and I was relieved. I will say there were moments when I considered calling my co-worker's room to help me get an ambulance and ride with me to a hospital (not where I wanted to go in a foreign country and only halfway through this two-leg business trip). You can call me crazy, but it did go away, and I finally fell asleep. I woke up early to my alarm, got up, felt fine, got ready, and headed to breakfast with my co-worker.

After almost a week in China, I was off to Egypt where I would be giving my presentation. I felt great and was very relieved the symptoms did not return. I made it to Cairo after a short layover in Bangkok, Thailand. I had quite an experience upon my arrival at Cairo airport. I had been informed that the Chinese CFO would meet me there to assist me in getting my visa, so that I could be released into the country. The CFO met me at my gate when I got off the plane. He took my passport from me and had me get in the security line. He executed some kind of transaction, and the security guard waived me through.

Visas are not issued in advance for Egypt. You must get them upon arrival. The CFO introduced me to a security guard, who walked me to the taxi he had waiting for me. It was an eye-opening ride to the Ritz Carlton on the Nile, where I would be staying for the duration of the trip. The air smelled of smoke, and there was a lot of obvious damage to the city in places. When we finally arrived at the hotel, the taxi had to go through two heavily guarded and armed gates with dogs sniffing my luggage and taxi for explosives or other weapons. The security guard walked me to check-in and waited until I had my room key. I thanked him, and I made my way to my room.

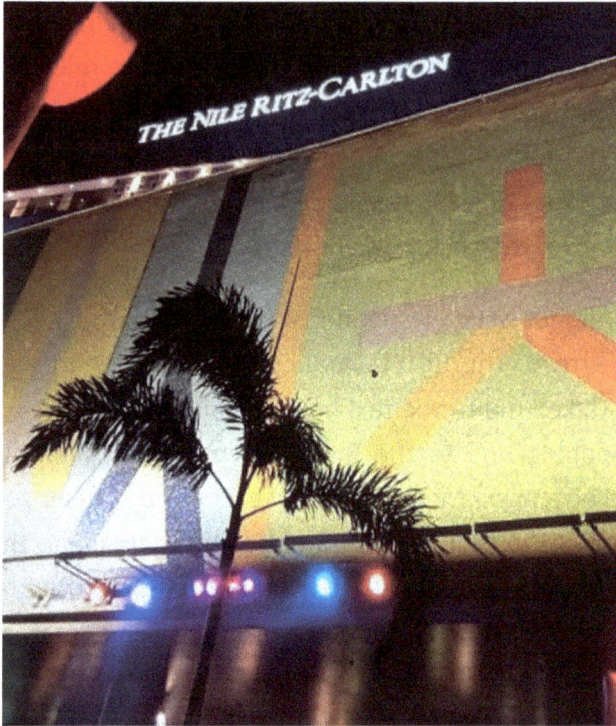

Figure 49: Company trip to Egypt. The Ritz Carlton on the Nile. Not your typical hotel. More like a city.

I will say this was the highlight hotel experience of my career, and I had travelled quite a bit over the years leading up to this. I was treated like royalty by the hotel staff. On a scale of one to ten, I would give them a 20. I had strict instructions to notify the security guard if I wanted to leave the hotel property. But who would need to leave? It was like a city there with multiple shops, restaurants, and basically anything you needed in the complex around the hotel. Plus, the food was amazing. It had been a long day of travel, so I met up with my CEO who had flown there from Tampa, and we had dinner. I was ready to end this day, so I made my way to my room for some much-needed rest. I do really wish that I had more time to schedule some sight-seeing, and maybe another time I'll get that opportunity, but we had a very tight schedule. The next day, the CEOs and I did our presentations and listened to all the other leaders who were presenting on behalf of their individual locations. I learned a lot about the new company from this trip, but I was ready to get home. I had been away for almost two weeks at this point. So, the CEO and I were homeward bound via a short layover in Paris (another place I hope to re-visit someday). Then, I was back in Tampa returning to the day-to-day.

Figure 50: Tallulah Gorge State Park, Georgia

Figure 51: Picture of Cairo from my room across the Nile.

CHAPTER 8

Returning To the Daily Grind, Or So I Thought

The very next morning, I was at the office early and making a telephone call to my cardiologist about the event I had experienced in China. He saw me the next day and, due to my existing heart issues, did an echocardiogram to assess what he could see based on the symptoms I described. He obviously could not tell me much because it had been well over a week since the event, but he did see some new damage to the heart muscle and wanted to monitor me more closely for a while. So, I agreed and back to work I went.

Life was finally back to the typical business, and I was hoping and praying that my major health issues were behind me. I was enjoying more good times with family now that I was feeling well again. I also had transitioned to an even healthier diet after the China-Egypt trip. I found a personal trainer and trimmed off the weight that accumulates naturally as we age and work in stressful job situations. To this day, I drink organic greens almost every day, eat grass fed/finished beef, and organic chicken. I also avoid white flour and sugar as much as I can to ward off disruptions to my health.

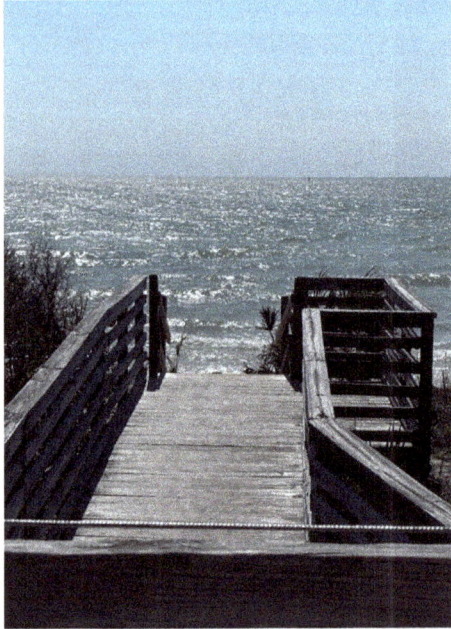

Figure 52: Dunedin Living – Caladesi Island

We did have some organizational changes happening at work, and I remained very busy during this time. It was stressful with the new owners and the changes they were making to the organization. In HR, we must be prepared at all times for the unexpected. Using this trait is, luckily, where I excelled. I worked on process improvement in all departments, engaging with each one to document their detailed processes. This project would take a year or two to get a good first draft review by those in each department. It was an important role where I had knowledge, specific training, and certification from an industry expert. It's not a typical HR responsibility, but I did this when I was in the citrus industry, so I didn't mind.

Since the engineers I had worked with had minimal time to document their processes, we used group meetings to document basic design, build processes, and assign certain tasks to individual engineers. We would then meet again to resolve questions or add missing pieces of each process. Utilizing this procedure provides great benefits to HR and the organization when recruiting to fill positions. You can't do an optimal hiring job without knowing at least the basic skills and behaviors required to complete the tasks for a specific job. Documented processes are also an invaluable tool to use for meeting required quality certification and training new employees. I loved this part of my job, but it always took time to get buy-in from department leaders who always had a lot on their plates. Selling this type of procedure to organization leaders is dependent on showing them the data that proves cost savings to the bottom line. If they choose to dedicate time to it, the procedure pays for itself quickly. Overall, they did a respectable job with the task. I want to believe it helped them in many ways.

In the fall of 2016, I was at work plugging along as I normally do. So much to do, and everything was a priority for the new Chinese owners. It is a different culture after all. I always poured everything into my work, and it was no different here. I had the added responsibility to control legal issues related to employee data transfers with the new owners who had no concept of privacy laws in the US. This was a learning curve for me since I had not worked previously within the Chinese work culture and their legal landscape. It was not always easy, and the task of educating them on requirements of U.S. law took a lot of time and energy.

I was home one evening and getting ready to go to bed after a busy week, and I was desperately in need of sleep. But no matter what I tried, I could not drift off. Once again, I began feeling pressure in my chest, and I was not able to lie down. Some indescribable, uncomfortable feeling kept me from lying down. Before I knew it, the clock said 5 a.m., or maybe even later. I began sweating profusely and was so weak I could barely walk. I got my phone and called my sister to take me to the hospital. She was always up early, and I thought she would be on her way to work soon. She quickly arrived to pick me up, and we were on our way. She dropped me at the ER and went to park her car. I walked in, and the reception nurse asked me how she could help. I told her I thought I was having a heart attack. No sooner were the words out of my mouth than a wheelchair was under my weak rear, taking me to a room where a half dozen people were putting IVs in my arm, attaching the electrocardiogram (EKG) sensors, and drawing blood. It was all a blur. After my sister came into the room, the doctor told us he felt strongly that it was a heart attack after looking at the EKG. My sister stayed with me until this point and then left to go to work with the assurance that I would let her know as soon as they had bloodwork results and knew anything more. I don't know what I would have done without her that day. She is the best sister I could ask for!

Long story short, the bloodwork confirmed that it was indeed a heart attack. I made a few phone calls to my daughters and my sister telling them the doctor would be doing a heart catheterization. I let my CEO know I'd be out for a few days for a medical emergency. Dianna arrived at the hospital just prior to the procedure. I was then wheeled to the operating room where my cardiologist's vascular surgeon on staff did the heart catheterization and found a blockage in my right coronary artery. He placed a stent in the artery to relieve the problem, and I went back to my room. Apparently, the right coronary artery was a tough spot that could easily become blocked, even after I'd switched to a healthier lifestyle. I was fortunate that the rest of my arterial system was in overall good condition, except for my right coronary artery. It could have been much worse.

Figure 53: This orchid was the start of my collection more than 15 years ago, a Yellow Dendrobium still growing on my patio.

CHAPTER 9

Retirement & Cancer

Life went forward for the next five years with the normal day-to-day. There was no shortage of things to do. I was now thinking about getting a plan in place for my future retirement. I had planned to retire by age fifty-five, but that didn't happen due to the fluctuating nature of the economy, an open project that I needed to complete, and my health issues. Now, it became necessary to make some adjustments. I shifted my retirement goal to age sixty and started planning.

By this time, I had been with the water treatment company for about six years and decided to move back to my home in Clearwater. As part of my future retirement plan, I wanted to begin some much-needed renovation of the home to prepare to sell it. I completed the work with the help of my daughters and put the house on the market about a year prior to my retirement. It sold in a week with a full cash offer and a little extra for some items the buyer wanted to purchase. The buyer wanted to close in two weeks. Great news, but it was going to be a tough timeline. I wasn't expecting to make the move so quickly. I had been house hunting and luckily had an offer accepted for a new home (my current home). Aligning the closing dates was tricky. I closed on my new home and moved in just days before closing on my previous home. Now, I had only a few days to clean the old home, so it was ready for the new owners to take possession. I was finally moved in and loved my new place. It needed a makeover, and so I did another renovation. This took some time, but I love this place and am so happy to be here.

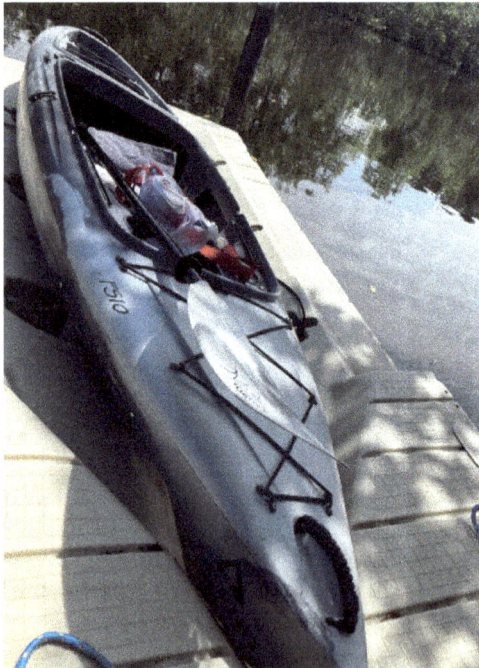

Figure 54: My personal boat slip at my retirement home. Easy to see why it feels like Paradise! A 5-minute paddle to St. Joseph's Sound.

One evening, in June of 2022, I was at home experiencing severe pain in my upper abdomen. I was sweating profusely and had no idea what was causing it. I called Dianna and told her I needed to get some kind of treatment. The pain was unbearable, and I couldn't do anything to make it go away. We went immediately to an urgent care facility. I was seen quickly, bloodwork was completed again, and it indicated another possible heart attack. According to my research, when one is having a heart attack, a component called troponin shows up in the blood. Since my history included a previous heart attack, this was their suspicion for the cause of my symptoms. Once they saw the bloodwork results, I was taken from urgent care to the closest hospital by ambulance. I again went through the process to identify exactly what was causing my symptoms. Fortunately, I was not having another heart attack, but they were not able to identify anything that could be causing this episode. I was given pain medication, and the pain was resolved. Then, they wanted to do a scan. I had a computed tomography (CT) scan done, and it showed I had a very large mass in my left lung. "Oh God, please help," is all I remember thinking. They did not believe it was related to the abdominal pain, but they were not certain. They were ready to do more scans. I pushed back, knowing full well I needed to get out of there and find a pulmonary specialist who could guide me through this next huge nightmare.

I knew I could do scans as an outpatient and save some money. It also did not make sense to do scans at the hospital when I was pretty sure the pulmonary doctor would want their own specific scans. Each doctor has their own preference for the protocol they use to complete their portion of the preliminary processes with a cancer diagnosis. Besides, everything is more expensive in the hospital, and I'd have to stay at least another night there. Why waste money on scans here that may not be useful to the next doctor I need to see? After all, I had prior medical incidents that I was trying to pay off. Health insurance is critical and absorbs a good portion of the cost with this type of thing, but we all know the deductibles, copays, and out of pocket max is an enormous burden that falls onto the patient. By this time, I was already expecting that I would be paying this off for the rest of my life. My entire HR career included managing benefits in addition to all the other HR responsibilities, so I had a lot of knowledge as to how to save money and time on this frightening surprise event.

The hospital staff tried to convince me to stay but finally released me to go home with a promise to schedule a follow-up with my primary care doctor, which I did immediately. I also began a research project to find the best pulmonary doctor in the Tampa Bay area. I found one of the best and continued to see him for follow-up appointments.

This doctor was amazing. He was instrumental in the process of assessing me, setting me up for procedures to measure lung function, and scheduling procedures for biopsies of the mass in my lung. He did all this while exuding a very positive mindset. This was encouraging for me since I had yet to go through the diagnosis process. Although he was very encouraging, he was also completely honest regarding the serious nature of the situation and did not sugar-coat anything. I appreciate that in a doctor.

The timing of meeting this doctor was beneficial for my mindset. I was struggling at this point and was so overwhelmed, to put it mildly. The doctor took the time to talk with me about how difficult this process could be, and this prompted me to realign my thoughts back to thinking positively. I had to surrender my fear and make a decision. I would not take on a victim mentality. As I saw it, I had two choices. Get my head straight and think positively, so I could do the work to research what would help me to beat this, or give up and die. Well, I was not ready to give up, so I got to work. Miracles do happen every day.

The doctor referred me to an excellent specialty surgeon who cleared the left lung of inflammation, took some biopsies, and removed a small piece of the malignant mass that was starting to invade the bronchial tube in my left lung. He then sealed it off to prevent further intrusion. These doctors, and there were several over the period from June through August 2022, were nothing short of wonderful. The biopsy results confirmed the mass was malignant, and they said it was stage four. This news was devastating. I found an amazing oncologist who jumped into action to get up to speed and start my treatment.

Following a CT scan, magnetic resonance imaging (MRI), a brain scan, a positron emission tomography (PET) scan, and further biopsies of the lymph glands in and around the lung, my oncologist downgraded me to stage three as my lymphatic system was negative for cancer (one of God's many miracles in my life). The oncologist developed a treatment plan that would begin in August and included thirty-three radiation treatments (one treatment each weekday, excluding holidays) and seven chemotherapy treatments (one each week in addition to radiation). It was a schedule that was overwhelming at the time. My treatment began right away.

In October 2022, when I was only a month into my cancer treatment plan, I suddenly found myself sweating with a fever, along with other symptoms. I thought it was due to the treatments. I called my sister that night, who picked me up and drove me to the closest hospital near my home, where I was admitted immediately. The staff believed my symptoms were not related to my cancer treatment at all. What it did show was a serious bile leak, a large cyst in my liver, pancreas, and entire abdominal area. I was diagnosed with acute sepsis. They gave me large doses of antibiotics to get the infection under control, and I spent five days in this hellish hospital on the psych/hospice floor. The infection required me to have a drain tapped into my liver, which was unbelievably painful, to drain all the infectious fluid and bile from my liver.

My wallet was also stolen during this stay. My sister checked for it in the ER, and checked the lost and found, but no such luck. My cash was gone, and it was not any fun cancelling all my cards, replacing my concealed carry permit, etc., as if I didn't have enough on my mind. My belongings were never recovered. I had forty dollars in that wallet, and I guess someone really needed those forty dollars, but then they most likely just tossed my other belongings into a trash can somewhere. Who knows! I hope it helped them at least.

Finally, I was released from the hospital, and Dianna brought me home. I will not make the mistake again of going to that hospital. It was a complete nightmare, but in this situation, I had no other choice. I thanked Dianna for all her help, and I thanked God for getting me back to my comfortable home. I don't think I had ever been more grateful to be home as I was that evening. As Dianna and I sat on the patio talking, I could not hold back the happy tears I was feeling. I will never go back there willingly.

In December of 2022, I had an appointment to follow-up with my surgeon and assess progress. He had previously attempted to repair the leaky bile duct with an endoscopic procedure. Unfortunately, it was unsuccessful. This meant I would need to have a more invasive surgery to repair it. We also were to discuss results of the MRI to decide on a plan to address the liver cyst they had found during a recent hospitalization. The infection was under control. This was a relief, but now I would be scheduled for major surgery. The goal would be to correct the leaky bile duct, remove a portion of the liver to get to the cyst, and attempt to remove it.

This was a tough surgery. The surgeon was able to repair the bile duct. He also had to remove 40% of my liver to get to the cyst. He was able to remove about half of the cyst, but the remainder would have to wait. I had been under anesthesia for a long time already, and I had already received two blood transfusions. He took biopsies of the cyst for testing and ended the surgery. The next morning when he did his rounds, he told me all of this. He said the remainder of the cyst was located close to the blood supply in the liver, so it would be tedious and slow work to get it out. Being that I had already been under so long the previous day, and removing the rest would have caused a great deal of bleeding, he would wait to see the biopsy results, and we would discuss it on the next visit. I went home a few days later to begin my healing process. The recovery was rough. The surgeon was honest about how full recovery from this surgery would take at least nine to twelve months. My body was already in a weakened state from my recent cancer treatment. I was not surprised. This surgery required me to have drains in my liver and abdomen when I went home, so I would need to schedule a follow-up appointment.

My follow-up appointment went well. I was making progress, although still moving around slowly. The good news was that the cyst was benign and had reduced in size somewhat since surgery. The bile duct repair was looking good, so we would do another MRI to look at progress in three months. To date, the remainder of the cyst continues to shrink.

Once I completed the chemotherapy and radiation treatment for cancer in November of 2022, it was determined that the mass was clear of any signs of cancer.

The radiation had turned the mass into scar tissue that would remain there. My tumor had not been operable due to being too close to the pericardial wall. I would now need to schedule monthly immunotherapy infusions. This practice had been showing encouraging results in preventing future recurrence of this type of cancer, according to my oncologist. I completed these treatments in November of 2023.

None of these issues would have been easy on their own, but I was not finished with my litany of surprises related to this saga. Since the completion of all the cancer treatment, I am still being monitored for the liver cyst and bile duct repair. I still suffer periodically from nausea, intermittent abdominal pain, and have had three hospitalizations, first with pneumonia and two with pancreatitis, which is not unusual with all that my body has endured over the past couple of years. I am healing, though. I had an MRI in July of 2024 and another in October to check on the process. It looks like the healing is progressing, but since there is no medicine to correct it, it is a slow process. I am scheduled in January 2025 to see a specialist to repair an old hernia that has become an aggravation to the repaired bile duct. This will be a laparoscopic repair I'll need to do soon, since my surgeon believes it may be contributing to the abdominal pain that comes and goes. The hernia has been there for years, so this was not a surprise.

The entire last three years have gone by so fast but were the most difficult times of my life. I had some very severe moments where I was at my lowest, but my daughters were both very supportive. Dianna lives locally, and she took on a lot of additional responsibility during this time, running me to appointments, cleaning the house for me, and adjusting her work schedule to be with me for each surgery through most of this frightening journey. We kept Jenn up to date with each step. I am sure she would rather have been here to help. She did take some vacation time and came to stay with me for a week or so during my treatment. I'm sure Dianna was grateful for the break. I also feel that Jenn's visit gave her some comfort knowing that, although I was weak and sick at times during treatment, I was doing ok. I am grateful to them both, and I have no idea how I would have survived without them. Thank you, my dear girls, you are God's greatest gifts to me!

Figure 55: Dianna and Jenn

CHAPTER 10

Resources and Helpful Tips

Following is a list of the tools I have found useful over the years when faced with difficult situations. I prepared this list to make it easier for others to navigate their own issues. It's tailored to address medical situations, since that was my focus, but it will work for any major challenge in life. You can always add to the list or ignore tools that don't work for your situation. This is just a starting point. There are many models for dealing with major change, grief, or challenges. For instance, in organizations where major changes are coming, companies typically seek guidance, well in advance, from experts on how to handle communicating upcoming changes to leadership. However, my situation was unique. I prepared this resource based on the needs I experienced going through my treatment. Feel free to use it, or research other change models that may help you. I found it a critical missing piece I needed at the time. I hope you never need it, but if you do, this will hopefully save you time and be an important tool if major life issues arise.

The basics:

Shock-> Denial-> Anger-> Acceptance-> Action

Deal With the Shock

No matter the situation, initially, most difficulties begin with receiving the news. At this time in the process, it's critical to take time to let the news settle. Shock is the first hurdle. This stage did not last very long for me, and I was quickly trying to search for reasons the result could be wrong. I knew at this point I was already moving into denial.

Denial

During this stage, it's normal to question the validity of the event you're going through. This stage was very short for me as well. It's hard to argue with science. I had test results that wouldn't let me deny reality for long. Sometimes this is a stage where a decent therapist can help to keep you from getting stuck in denial. For me, it was dealing with the fear of the situation and what "could" be driving that fear.

Anger

Anger is tied closely with denial. It happens almost in sync with denial. This stage is when you question: why me? It can easily suck you into being a victim to your situation. Instead of succumbing to this anger, you can use positive thinking to quickly move on to the next stage. It may be helpful to find a safe way to express your anger. Yell, throw something, cry, pound your fist on the table. Just be safe and try not to hurt yourself or others with physical or verbal expressions. It's critical to know that what you are going through emotionally is completely normal. The timing and process can be different for each person, but the important thing is having a process to guide you. Face it, and know that it is okay to go there, just don't stay there too long. This is especially important in medical situations. Time can make or break your potential situation for beating cancer, for instance. Let yourself go through it naturally, but not for too long.

Acceptance

This is when you've freed yourself of limiting beliefs, and you're ready to do something about it. In fact, for me, it was the shortest stage—from a time perspective. I was developing a plan, immediately, by the time I hit the stage of acceptance. I knew research was where I should start. I needed to know the process for determining the next steps of the treatment. Be sure to ask questions of experts in the field your unique situation falls into. In other words, get your ducks in a row.

Action

Here are additional steps I found helpful when researching that were important and relevant in my situation:

Support Community:

Share your situation with family and close friends. These are most likely the people who will make up a good portion of your support system. They will be helpful with what you need. A few things they may be able to help with are rides if you can't drive, picking up groceries, assisting with household chores, etc. Those close to you will want to help, but you'll need to ask for and accept their help. Maybe your community includes a book club, a church group, or volunteer activities. These are just a few of many options, but any of them would be good groups from which to build your community.

See if there are any support groups that may help with your situation. These types of groups can be so helpful because others in similar situations may provide information that saves you time in your process development.

Maintain a Positive Mindset:

Our brains are the most powerful tool we have. How you think and speak to yourself, and others, will have an impact on the outcome of any situation. It is normal to have negative thoughts now and then. We are all human after all. But it's important to try and combat that with positive thoughts.

Utilize Research Skills:

No matter the type of situation, you will have to obtain knowledge to help you make your way through the process. For instance, when I received my cancer diagnosis, I had no idea how to approach it. What do I do first? Who do I go to first? "Talk with your primary care doctor, they may have a recommendation," I thought. Well, that clearly didn't work out for me. A nurse at the hospital told me about her dad's recent situation with cancer. She indicated that I should start with a pulmonary specialist. This prompted me to go to Google. You may use a different search engine. Simply search for what you want to see. I searched "top 10 pulmonologists in the Tampa area."

I read the reviews—all of them (as many as they had). I watched any physician videos they had posted. This helped me identify if the doctors had good communication skills, good bedside manner, etc., and ultimately if I felt we would mesh with each other.

I reviewed education, medical specialties, and internships. For my situation, I wanted the best doctor with the right credentials. I chose my top two and scheduled consultations to meet with them personally. Take good notes during these conversations. I created labels and applied a point system to each factor. Factors I used for my labels are below this paragraph. You can use them or ignore them. After the fact, my notes provided a system that validated my gut feelings or gave me a reason to challenge the doctors. You may or may not need this step.

Factors: Degree, College attended, Hospital where they completed their residency, Demeanor, Level of interest, Thoroughness of answers, Other (for my situation, this factor was whether my pulmonologist knew them and what his thoughts were about the two oncologists I consulted with following my research).

Be sure to start a journal right in the beginning so you can note the dates of each action from this point forward until your situation is complete. Unfortunately, I didn't start my journal right away. This was a lesson learned for me. My notes were not extensive enough in the beginning, so I had some gaps and could not remember all the details.

Overall, following these steps allowed me to make a good decision. They were especially important for finding specialty doctors like my oncologist and my surgeons. This was how I found my starting point.

So, use Safari, Google, etc., and make yourself a junior expert on whatever issue you're facing and ask a lot of questions. Research the overall process related to your situation. Ask your first point of contact to outline the general process. My pulmonologist gave me a document that showed the steps since he had many of his patients ask about this. Then, look at the steps in the process, document them, and check them off as you obtain the knowledge.

Nutrition/Diet

Many of us are actively eating healthier these days. I have been for over fifteen years. Obviously, it does not prevent everything, but your body needs healthy fuel to heal from disease or illness. It is especially important for those of us who have worked in stressful jobs or dealt with a lot of personal anxiety. Below, I provided a list of the primary things I changed about my diet.

Consume pasture raised meats that are U.S. grown. Beef that was specifically grass-fed and finished, chicken that is free-range and no hormones; I prefer uncured, hormone-free pork. I prefer USDA organic produce and non-GMO labels for foods and for snacks. I try to avoid eating processed foods. I have replaced white flour with almond flour for cooking and baking, and I avoid low-fat foods due to what food companies replace the fat with when they process their products (like yogurt, milk, salad dressings, etc.). I try to choose foods that are naturally lower in bad fats. I prefer to manage flavor with spices and eat a reasonable amount of good fats like coconut oil, avocado oil, or olive oil. I eat very little sugar. I use monk fruit or agave as my go-to sweeteners. I bake a lot and love chocolate, so I use dark chocolate with a high cacao content. I like the bitterness of dark chocolate. I use the air fryer for much of my cooking, and I avoid fried foods when possible. I eat slowly so I can tell when I'm full and need to stop eating. My portion sizes are probably half what they were previously. If I crave something, I have it. My approach is not to deprive myself but to maintain healthy choices most of the time. You can choose what you prefer. But just do the best you can. If change is hard for you, try changing one thing at a time.

Exercise - Move Your Body

Your body needs to be strong. Food is only part of keeping your health in check. Make sure you get plenty of rest, but try not to lay around all day; although I found some days were better than others, so try not to be too hard on yourself. With the right fuel (foods) in your body, you will be able to build lean muscles to keep your body strong. In my situation, I could not exercise much during treatment, so I lost a lot of my muscle tone. I don't need crazy workouts every day. I tend to consider all activities that keep me moving as exercise. Housework, walking to get my mail, or taking my trash out all count as a physical workout to me. I have been recovering from an unprecedented issue recently, so I'm not back up to walking 10,000 steps a day yet, but I'm making progress. My personal favorite exercises are walking, kayaking, hiking, chair and wall Pilates, and yoga; all low-impact exercises. I only exercise three times a week maximum. I make sure to have at least one day in between, because your body needs rest. Just remember that the more you move following surgery or a hospitalization, the faster you will recover and get your strength back.

Strengthen Your Mind

I choose to read, play solitaire, and write. I read different types of literature ranging from news to novels to medical journals and articles. This keeps your mind active and increases knowledge. This was important for me due to chemotherapy, as it impacted my short-term memory a bit. It also is a great de-stressor because when I focus on a book or article, I'm not thinking about my worries. I meditate, usually in the morning, but some days in both the morning and evening. This gives me a chance to set my intentions and begin or end my day on a positive note. I listen to music when I do housework or laundry. Music brings back memories from the past and that fills me with joy. It also helps with passing the time while completing tasks or just relaxing. It also can serve as a good form of exercise. You may like to dance around your house to the music. Great! Whatever makes you happy.

Do not hesitate to fall back on your own family, close friends, or outside resources to help you through the muddy process and down the path toward success at survival. You will need them. They will willingly and selflessly stand by your side if you ask, and you should not hesitate to do so. I am forever grateful to all of those who supported me throughout these past few years. I've thanked most of you personally for your sacrifices and loyalty. Trust me, I felt the love.

Lean on your own strength and those around you that love and care for you. It will be critical for your survival.

Do not hesitate to use therapy. It amazes me that people still have a stigma about getting mental health support. I have no shame that this has been helpful for me at times to keep my head on straight and keep a positive attitude (although Dianna & Jennifer can tell you, I had many cracks in my armor throughout this nightmare). I was angry and felt I was being punished many times at the start, but this is where my faith stepped in to back me up. So, whatever tools you have, use them all, never give up, and just fight like hell.

FINAL THOUGHTS

My Secret Superpower

I love to believe I have a superpower, but with all honesty, it's my faith. I have to give the credit to God himself. He is my strength in times of trouble. I cannot grasp how anyone gets through life without God at their side. He knows I'm strong, but He gave me that strength. He knows I'm stubborn, but He created me intentionally this way because He knew it's how I would need to be. He knew I was resilient, disciplined, and a real fighter, and He knew all of this because he infused my being with all the tools that He knew I would need to get through this life. So, thank you God for standing by me and carrying me through when I could not do it on my own. You are my God, my hero, my Savior!

I wanted to share this story, though it is very personal to me. I have only confided to a small number of people what I've been going through—until now. Sharing my story forced me well outside my comfort zone. I'm doing it now because I know time will blur the memories, and as much as this has been a difficult journey, it is not one I want to forget. I believe that I am not the only one who has faced such challenges as well. Perhaps this helps someone as a result. I hope it will inspire you and encourage you to get out your tools. My tools are faith and all those amazing traits God gave me, but each of you have your own tools, beliefs, and traits that you may need when facing your own personal challenges. So, get them out and be prepared to use them all.

Figure 56: Bird in Flight, St. Joseph's Sound

EPILOGUE

As of writing this, it is January of 2025. I've now completed 18 months cancer-free. I currently have a CT scan and bloodwork every three months to check my progress since completing my cancer treatment. I'm happy and very grateful to report that I have been doing well. I am still cancer free. It hasn't been long though, so I will be diligent in following up as recommended by my oncologist to stay on top of my health. I'm still being monitored for the liver, pancreas issue, and bile duct. I am cautiously optimistic at this time because the pancreas shows continued healing, and the cyst is still shrinking. It now seems the bile duct is doing well, and I still need to have the hernia repaired. I have seen the specialty surgeon and will most likely have this done soon.

My intent from the beginning has been to help others overcome their own challenges by offering encouragement and hope. The tools provided will help no matter what the situation. I hope my efforts prove successful.

Today, I feel amazing. I have been working out again, and I am almost 100%. I've been out on the water in my kayak, getting back to nature in the Gulf. Being in nature always feeds me and is extra special for me when it includes the ocean. I was raised on the Gulf of Mexico, and I will take every opportunity to go again and again. My energy isn't quite up to my norm, and I am still exhausted a bit after kayaking, but I sit on my patio in my little personal piece of paradise and thank my Maker each time for providing the strength for me to get past so many obstacles.

I am expecting many new adventures soon, and I have zillions of new memories to make. I'm starting that bucket list and getting busy scheduling some well-deserved adventures. God willing, I may just write another book to share all those adventures with you. For now, I'm going to focus on enjoying every adventure and living in the moment.

Good luck with your struggles and stay strong!

ABOUT THE AUTHOR

Gail was born in Maine, the second of three children, and lived there with her family until age nine. Her family moved to Florida in 1969 and originally settled in New Port Richey, later moving to Dunedin with her family. She spent the remainder of her school years in Dunedin and graduated from Dunedin High School. She attended St. Petersburg Junior College, majoring in Business Administration until the birth of her two daughters.

Gail's career was spent initially in multiple business administrative positions, leading to more than 40 years in human resources (HR) leadership roles. She has extensive HR experience in the citrus, automotive, communications print/media, and water treatment plant design/build industries. Gail retired from the working world in 2020 and did some minor consulting work for a year or so. Gail currently resides in Pinellas County, happily living on the water, where her heart feels at home again.

Gail has traveled extensively, either for work or pleasure in the U.S., the Bahamas, Jamaica, Europe, South Korea, China, and Egypt.

Gail has always been passionate about her faith, family, gardening, photography, and nature. She enjoys spending time biking, traveling, and on the ocean kayaking, fishing or just boating in general. She shares that she has enjoyed writing throughout her life. From writing about summer vacations during elementary school to writing poetry, short stories, and essays, her passion for writing continued to grow.

With her working life behind her, she has taken this opportunity to write and publish a very personal story with the original intention of creating a keepsake for her daughters and grandchildren following major obstacles in her life. In the process of writing this story, she felt inspired to publish it. By sharing her story with others who may be experiencing their own obstacles, she felt that it may give someone hope and resilience to push through when they feel like giving up.

The author can be contacted at <u>Gail-G-Dove@hotmail.com</u> for speaking engagements, book signings and interviews.

www.ingramcontent.com/pod-product-compliance
Lightning Source LLC
Chambersburg PA
CBHW071945100426
42736CB00042B/2075